CHAKRAS FOR BEGINNERS

A COMPLETE GUIDE TO OPEN, BALANCE, AND HEAL YOUR CHAKRAS FOR POSITIVE ENERGY

KAREN NGUYEN

© **Copyright 2021 - All rights reserved.**

The content contained within this book may not be reproduced, duplicated, or transmitted without direct written permission from the author or the publisher.

Under no circumstances will any blame or legal responsibility be held against the publisher, or author, for any damages, reparation, or monetary loss due to the information contained within this book, either directly or indirectly.

Legal Notice:

This book is copyright protected. It is only for personal use. You cannot amend, distribute, sell, use, quote, or paraphrase any part, or the content within this book, without the consent of the author or publisher.

Disclaimer Notice:

Please note the information contained within this document is for educational and entertainment purposes only. All effort has been executed to present accurate, up-to-date, reliable, complete information. No warranties of any kind are declared or implied. Readers acknowledge that the author is not engaged in the rendering of legal, financial, medical, or professional advice. The content within this book has been derived from various sources. Please consult a licensed professional before attempting any techniques outlined in this book.

By reading this document, the reader agrees that under no circumstances is the author responsible for any losses, direct or indirect, that are incurred as a result of the use of the information contained within this document, including, but not limited to, errors, omissions, or inaccuracies.

CONTENTS

Book Description	7
Introduction	9
1. UNDERSTANDING CHAKRAS	13
A Short History	14
The Energy Systems	16
The Energy Bodies	22
The Transpersonal Chakras	25
Adaptations of the Chakra System	27
The Western Scientific Take on Chakras	29
Conflicting Opinions About Chakras	30
2. THE ROOT CHAKRA—THE FOUNDATION	33
Summary	34
Understanding the Root Chakra	35
The Spiritual Law Governing the Root Chakra	36
What Can Block the Root Chakra?	36
Signs of an Unbalanced Root Chakra	37
Restoring Balance and Healing the Root Chakra	37
3. THE SACRAL CHAKRA—WHERE THE SELF DWELLS	59
Summary	59
The Sanskrit Name	60
Understanding the Sacral Chakra	61
The Spiritual Law Governing the Sacral Chakra	62
What Can Block the Sacral Chakra?	62
Signs of an Unbalanced Sacral Chakra	63
Restoring Balance and Healing the Sacral Chakra	63

4. THE SOLAR PLEXUS CHAKRA—A LUSTROUS GEM 84
   Summary 84
   The Sanskrit Name 85
   Understanding the Solar Plexus Chakra 87
   The Spiritual Law Governing the Solar Plexus Chakra 87
   What Can Block the Solar Plexus Chakra? 87
   Signs of an Unbalanced Solar Plexus Chakra 88
   Restoring Balance and Healing the Solar Plexus Chakra 88

5. THE HEART CHAKRA—THE UNBEATEN 108
   Summary 108
   The Sanskrit Name 109
   Understanding the Heart Chakra 111
   The Spiritual Law Governing the Heart Chakra 111
   What Can Block the Heart Chakra? 111
   Signs of an Unbalanced Heart Chakra 112
   Restoring Balance and Healing the Heart Chakra 112

6. THE THROAT CHAKRA—THE PURIFIER 130
   Summary 130
   The Sanskrit Name 131
   Understanding the Throat Chakra 132
   The Spiritual Law Governing the Throat Chakra 133
   What Can Block the Throat Chakra? 133
   Signs of an Unbalanced Throat Chakra 133
   Restoring Balance and Healing the Throat Chakra 134

7. THE THIRD EYE CHAKRA—THE BRIDGE 149
   Summary 149
   The Sanskrit Name 150
   Understanding the Third Eye Chakra 151
   The Spiritual Law Governing the Third Eye Chakra 152
   What Can Block the Third Eye Chakra? 152
   Signs of an Unbalanced Third Eye Chakra 153
   Restoring Balance and Healing the Third Eye Chakra 153

8. THE CROWN CHAKRA—THE INFINITE	167
Summary	167
The Sanskrit Name	168
Understanding the Crown Chakra	169
The Spiritual Law Governing the Crown Chakra	170
What Can Block the Crown Chakra?	170
Signs of an Unbalanced Crown Chakra	171
Restoring Balance and Healing the Crown Chakra	171
Conclusion	185
References	187

BOOK DESCRIPTION

Ever since the western world learned about chakras during the previous century, interest in the concept has grown. Today, there are numerous alternative health practitioners engaged in balancing and opening chakras, and there is a proliferation of information available on the Internet.

It is a wide field with many facets that can be confusing to a beginner. This book takes the reader step-by-step through the chakra system.

The short history puts the origins of the chakra teachings into perspective. Basic esoteric concepts that are relevant to the chakra system are also explained in simple, understandable terms.

In the subsequent chapters, the chakras are discussed, one by one, in detail. Several practical steps and exercises are provided to help readers keep their chakras functioning optimally.

The easy instructions for several yoga poses are a bonus.

This book is a treasure trove of information and practical applications, invaluable to every student of the chakra system.

INTRODUCTION

Emotions are always reflected in our bodies.

"Emotion always has its roots in the unconscious and manifests itself in the body."

— IRENE CLAREMONT DE CASTILLEJO

Emotions and the feelings they evoke are fully intertwined with the sensations we experience in our bodies. In ancient medicine, such as Traditional Chinese Medicine, the link was acknowledged centuries ago and treatments were designed according to the wisdom.

It is only in the last decades that western science also started serious investigations into the relationship between some of our modern ailments and the emotions we experience. Even more important are the feelings we repress, that find their expression in physical manifestations throughout the body.

WHO IS KAREN NGUYEN?

The author of this treasure trove of wisdom and information you are reading right now is a single woman on a spiritual journey to uncover metaphysical secrets.

Karen Nguyen holds a Bachelor's degree in Environmental Studies from San Jose State University. She spends all her free time studying the principle of metaphysics and has been immersed in its secrets since 2018.

"I am passionate about sharing my passion and knowledge with others on the same quest. I regularly practice the exercises in this book myself and know from experience that they can make a huge difference in anyone's life.

"It is my wish that the information in this book will help you to achieve balanced, open, and healed chakras. I know how profound the difference will be for you because I have personally been on the same spiritual journey."

Let's dive right into the fascinating world of chakras!

1

UNDERSTANDING CHAKRAS

The locations of all the chakras.

Chakras have become, at the same time, one of the best-known, and also one of the most misunderstood concepts in alternative therapies. Many people talk about chakras without understanding the full scope and importance of these energy centers.

In this chapter, we'll unpack the basics of chakras. Where it started, what they are exactly, and how they should be cared for.

A SHORT HISTORY

The concept of a king that turns his empire like a wheel from a center, representing power, comes from what is known as the Vedic time in India. This was between 1500 and 500 BCE. This was before the development of writing as we know it. The language spoken at that time was Sanskrit and the body of information was passed on from generation to generation in what is today called the Veda.

In later Vedic times, the Veda was put into writing. While some scholars believe there was no mention of chakras in a psychic-energy sense at that time, Hindu texts from the late Vedic period called the Upanishad talk about the nadis or energy channels for the first time (Feuerstein, 2003).

The first time chakras were written about as hierarchical centers of energy in the body was in about the eight century CE, in Buddhist texts called tantras. They speak of only four chakras at that stage.

Our modern word 'chakra' comes from the Sanskrit word 'cakra.' It means 'wheel' or 'circle.'

Chakras are focal points of energy in the body, pulling together organs and organ systems. There are 114 chakras, but seven of them are seen as the main centers. Two of the 114 chakras are outside the body. Of the remaining 112, only 108 can be worked on because the other four flourish as consequences of the rest of the chakras.

The 112 chakras are arranged into seven dimensions. Each dimension has 16 aspects. To make it easier to explain, a chakra was associated with each of the seven dimensions and these seven became what most modern people believe to be the only chakras.

Early Classifications

In early Hindu and Buddhist literature, chakras and nadis are seen as subtle energy bodies. They are invisible concepts that are essential for the life force, or prana, to flow.

Prana is far more complex than mere inhalation and exhalation—it is the essence of a human that leaves at the moment of death and only an empty physical body remains.

At this stage in Hindu and Buddhist spiritual literature, nadis and chakras were closely associated with emotions (New World Encyclopedia, 2021).

- **The Hindu tantra:** There are several systems of chakras. The six-plus-one model is most widely used. According to this classification, the six chakras work up from the bottom and culminate in the seventh that is called the crown or sahasrara. Starting from the lowest, or root, chakra, the six others are called the muladhara, svadhisthana (sacral), manipura (solar plexus), anahata (heart), vishuddhi (throat), and ajna (third eye).

The beliefs about the chakra system are embodied in a branch of Hinduism called Shaktism. They worship the goddess Shakti as the personification of primordial energy. Pure Shaktism adds two more chakras: the swadhisthana (tail bone, pertaining to unconscious desires) and bindu (a dot at the back of the head, pertaining to prayer) (New World Encyclopedia, 2021).

- **The Buddhist tantra:** Buddhist literature generally teaches four chakras. They are the manipura (navel), anahata (heart), vishuddha (throat), and ushnisha kamala (crown). The chakras are considered to be parallel to cosmic processes, each with a buddha as a counterpart (New World Encyclopedia, 2021).
- **Tibetan Buddhism:** They have a system of five chakras, being the navel, abdominal, heart, throat, and crown. Prana and chakras stand central in Buddhist practices in Tibet (New World Encyclopedia, 2021).

THE ENERGY SYSTEMS

In ancient times, it was believed that existence entails not only a physical body that has mass, but also an energy or subtle body that is emotional and non-physical. Whenever ailments and diseases struck the physical body, they looked for the cure in the non-physical body, believing an imbalance of some sort in the emotional body was to blame.

The emotional, or subtle, body is made up of energy systems that include the nadis (known as meridians in Traditional Chinese medicine), that are connected to each other by spinning nodes called chakras, and the auric layers.

Nadis/Meridians

Energy does not move randomly through the body; it follows fixed paths. These paths are called nadis, or channels. Traditional Chinese medicine (TCM) call them energy meridians.

In TCM, there are 12 meridians that are each connected to a specific organ or organ system. The meridians occur in pairs, with a yin meridian on one side of the body and a yang meridian on the other. Yin corresponds to cold and yang to heat (Fellows, n.d.).

On the side of the Vedic tradition, three main nadis out of the 72,000 that are believed to exist in the energy body of every human being are recognized. The three are called the pingala, ida, and sushumna.

The ida and pingala can be compared to the physical holes in the vertebrae on either side of the spine, where the nerves pass through. The space in the middle can be compared to the sushumna.

The ida and pingala are the male and female qualities that have to unite in the sushumna for a person to reach his/her full potential.

The ida is to the left of the sushumna and encompasses the feminine aspect. It starts at the root chakra and flows on the left side toward the left nostril.

The ida nadi is connected to the moon and controls mental processes, bringing calm, introversion, and creativity. The energy has to be balanced by the pingala on the right hand side.

The pingala is associated with masculine, analytical, and sometimes aggressive energy. It starts at the root chakra and runs to the right of the sushumna toward the right nostril.

It is also known as solar energy because of its association with the sun.

Dominance of the pingala brings the conviction that there is only one truth that dismisses any other beliefs, while dominance of the ida leads to the belief that all truths are equal. The ida and pingala have to meet each other in the sushumna to be truly effective in the world and achieve one's purpose in life.

Sushumna is neutral and does not change in response to the events of the outside world. It is always in perfect balance and harmony despite any turmoil around it. The ida and pingala, on the other hand, change to reflect the environment. They can be calm one moment and emotionally crazy the next.

Yogis believe the ida and pingala nadis have to be purified daily to ensure the energy enters into the sushumna. An easy way to do this is to practice alternate nostril breathing. One nostril is closed while a cycle of breathing in and out is completed. Then the process is repeated with the other nostril.

Auric Layers

An aura is the energy field that surrounds all living beings. It is an electro-magnetic force field that consists of seven layers, or planes, that each represent something specific. The purpose of the aura is to ward off potentially harmful vibrations.

The auric layers have the same colors as their corresponding chakras associated with them.

The seven are:

- **Physical:** It is the layer closest to the skin, relating to our physical condition.
- **Emotional:** The second layer responds to emotions, and changes color according to your mood. In times of emotional distress, the emotional layer appears smudged.
- **Mental:** The third layer is all about logic and reasoning.
- **Astral body:** This layer deals with spiritual health and holds a person's capacity to love.
- **Etheric:** Psychic abilities reside in the etheric layer.
- **Celestial:** Dreams and intuition live in the sixth layer. People with a healthy and strong celestial auric plane are often very creative.
- **Causal:** The seventh layer harmonizes all the other layers and acts as a guide on a person's life path.

The Modern Classification of Chakras

The seven chakras, or energy vortices, that we'll be working with in this book will be discussed in more detail in later chapters.

The western system of chakras consists of, in ascending order, the root, sacral, solar plexus, heart, throat, third eye, and crown chakras.

The top three are considered spiritual, and the lower three physical. The two parts are connected in the heart chakra.

Root Chakra or Muladhara

The root chakra relates to security, survival, and instincts. It also influences physical stability, and when it is blocked or inactive, a feeling of vertigo may result. When this chakra is overactive, the person may experience a sensation of stagnation in personal and interpersonal matters.

The Sanskrit word 'muladhara' means 'support.' When the root chakra is open and balanced, the person feels supported and can move confidently in the world, that is the physical realm we have to exist in too.

Sacral Chakra or Svadhisthana

The sacral chakra represents creativity and the life-giving force of creating something.

Imbalances or blockages can manifest in problems pursuing an artistic interest, lack of inspiration, or even physical infertility. It can also show a loss of desire for sexual intimacy.

Solar Plexus Chakra or Manipura

The third chakra is a keystone between the base chakras and the higher ones. It acts as a bridge, validating the creations of the second chakra and putting them to the uses required by the higher chakras. It provides a transition from simple emotions to more complex emotions.

Heart Chakra or Anahata

The center of the body's energy system lies in the heart chakra. It regulates the flow of energy like the physical heart regulates the flow of blood. When it is open and functioning as it should, the person is open to unconditional love for the self and others.

A blocked heart chakra can leave the person feeling without hope and in despair.

Throat Chakra or Vishuddha

Communication, growth, and speaking one's truth are all embodied in the throat chakra. Truth refers to both personal and collective truths.

Balancing and opening a blocked throat chakra can also heal old wounds of not feeling heard, sometimes stemming from childhood experiences.

Third Eye Chakra or Ajna (Agya)

The sixth chakra is associated with deep awareness and intuition, bringing wisdom.

When the third eye is blocked, it brings an intense sense of confusion and an inability to make sense of and focus on things around you. It often manifests with a vague sense of dissatisfaction that leads a person to ask if there is more to life than what they have been experiencing so far.

Crown Chakra or Sahasrara

Pulling all the other chakras together in consciousness, the crown chakra is located outside the body, above the head.

It is seen as the connection with the divine, creating intimate awareness of the nature of the source of all beings.

It can be described as an energy sanctuary for the mind.

THE ENERGY BODIES

Energy, or subtle, bodies have been known since ancient times. The earliest mention of subtle bodies is found in Chinese Taoist texts from the 2nd century BCE (Wang & Pregadio, 2011).

Esoteric writings recognize seven energy bodies. That is in contrast with the western mind-body dualistic viewpoint.

Western scientists have for years denied the existence of any type of body other than the physical because the subtle bodies can not be quantified in the same way physical matter can. The fact that the accounts of people who had near-death experiences and out-0f-body episodes are very similar, however, piqued scientific interest.

In 1933, the Swiss astronomer Fritz Zwicky discovered an anomaly in the mass of the stars in the Coma cluster of galaxies. He found that the recorded mass was only one percent of what was needed to keep the galaxies within the cluster's gravitational pull.

The reality of the "missing mass" was doubted for decades until two American astronomers confirmed the observation in the 1970s.

Scientists concluded there has to be mass that is not visible to our eyes and instruments. For want of a better term, they called this mass dark matter.

It has since been confirmed that dark matter makes up most of the universe. Furthermore, dark matter exists on its own and can move freely through physical matter without us being aware of it (Riess, 2019).

The existence of dark matter has led some scholars to conclude that it is scientific proof for the existence of subtle bodies (Kazanis, 1995).

The seven energy bodies that have been known since early times are the etheric, emotional, lower mental, higher mental, causal, soul, and integrated spiritual bodies.

The Etheric Body

The body closest to the physical body and also the densest of the seven energy bodies is called the etheric field. It contains the energy blueprint of the physical body. The nadis, chakras, and auras reside in the etheric body.

It vibrates at a slightly higher frequency than the physical and is linked to the base chakra.

The Emotional Body

The next layer is the emotional body. Our feelings and emotions reside there. The emotions create patterns that get stored there and determine our responses to events.

The emotional body functions outside of time. It is linked to the sacral chakra.

The Lower Mental Body

This body is where our mental processes and thoughts take place. The thoughts are powerful enough to reach outside the mental body. When a thought teams up with an emotion, we become creators. It is important to choose the thoughts we allow, carefully.

The lower mental body is linked to the solar plexus chakra.

The Higher Mental Body

This is the place where we receive insights from the spiritual realm. The higher mental body relates to the heart chakra and is the meeting point between the physical and soul energies.

Patterns from past lives are filtered here to allow only the important karmic information to come through into our present consciousness.

The Causal Body

The causal body acts as a doorway through which we can join the collective consciousness of humankind. It is depicted as seven concentric circles in the colors of the rainbow that contain our real essence. Talents and gifts brought through from previous lives are stored here.

This energy body is linked to the throat chakra, as well as the causal chakra at the back of the head.

The Soul Body

This is your link to the essence of the divine, the part of you that is pure spirit. Inspiration and information needed by the lower bodies are obtained here and filtered through to where they are needed.

The soul body is linked to the third eye chakra.

The Integrated Spiritual Body

The last energy body merges all the previous subtle bodies. It is linked to the crown chakra.

THE TRANSPERSONAL CHAKRAS

Besides the seven main physical chakras, there are five others that are considered as transpersonal.

In the 12-chakra system, the transpersonal chakras relate to the physical chakras and bring the dimension of transcendency to our earthly existence.

The Earth Star Chakra

It is an energy point situated about 12 inches below the feet. It forms a direct line with the root chakra and aligns us with the magnetic field of the earth.

The earth star point focuses our energy and grounds us.

The Navel Chakra

This chakra is situated below the navel in the auric field. It is not equivalent to the sacral chakra, but is between the sacral and solar plexus chakras.

It makes us aware of our true purpose and awakes the desire to live according to the divine will. It also relates to courage and strength.

The Thymus Chakra

The thymus energy point is also sometimes called the higher heart. It stimulates the desire to show compassion and helps us to experience unconditional love.

It plays an important role in unfolding and growing spiritually.

The Causal Chakra

The causal chakra is located three to four inches behind the center of the back of the head.

It brings the qualities of intuition and compassion.

The Soul Star

This energy point is above the crown chakra. It aligns the soul with the universe and allows the maximum amount of light and healing to reach us.

It makes us fully aware of our connection to the divine and empowers and enlightens us.

ADAPTATIONS OF THE CHAKRA SYSTEM

Chakras are central in the Hindu, Buddhist, and yogic traditions. Besides those groups, many other cultures also have some variation of the seven or 12-chakra-system (or something that can be construed as referring to chakras), even if it is not always called by that name.

Judaism

In the Kabbalah, which deals with concepts in Jewish mysticism, reference is made to spheres that represent the world and the energy of the human body. They are grouped in seven levels and mapped on the Tree of Life.

Christianity

Some scholars believe references to chakras are made in the Bible. The instances mentioned include Jacob's dream about a ladder he climbed from the earth to heaven, and certain passages in the book of Revelation.

Islam

The esoteric branch of Islam called Sufism recognizes the existence of sensory portals in the body that act as energy centers. They are called lataif (singular latifa) and each one corresponds to a color, organ, and Muslim prophet.

Traditional Chinese Medicine

In Traditional Chinese Medicine (TCM) chakras are called dantians. They consist of energy centers known in TCM as the Three Treasures: Jing (generating energy), qi (vital energy), and shen (spirit). Each dantian has an upper, middle, and lower center.

Japan

The energy healing system known as Reiki, which originated in Japan, also works with chakras as focal points for energy.

The full chakra system was added in the 1980s. In the original teachings, Reiki practitioners only worked with what is known in Japan and China as the hara, which is the chakra situated under the navel.

The Mayans

Studies of the imagery used in Mayan culture reveals many symbols that remind of chakras, as well as the idea of central energy in the form of a serpent, as believed in kundalini yoga traditions. Mayan priests seem to have practiced yoga in the same way it was done in India.

The Aboriginal Traditions

The Aboriginal system of chakras is closely linked to the use of the didgeridoo, a type of flute made from a hollowed out tree trunk. Many of their healing rituals and ceremonies use the music of the didgeridoo to center on energy vortices throughout the body.

Native Americans

Energy fields that surround the body and energy centers that focus the fields are well-known to many native American tribes. One such tribe is the Pueblos, who refer to spiritual centers in various places in the body. Each center relates to an organ.

THE WESTERN SCIENTIFIC TAKE ON CHAKRAS

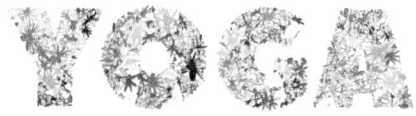

Some people use yoga as an attempt to find a physical relationship between our bodies and chakras.

Various western scholars have tried to give a scientific basis to the chakra system. Some have worked from a physiological perspective, while others have approached the subject purely from a psychological viewpoint.

The underlying problem with all these models is that western science starts mostly from a separated body/mind model. The eastern take on the makeup of human beings integrates the physical aspects with mind, soul, and spirit.

Psychologist Dr. Richard Maxwell (2009) proposed a model linking chakras to gap junctions between cells in the body. Gap junctions are specialized connection points, or gates, that allow electrical impulses, ions, and various molecules to pass directly between cells. According to Maxwell's theory, the physical locations of the chakras are places in the body where there is a proliferation of gap junctions. He further theorized that these high-density areas are formed during embryological development.

In other models, chakras have been aligned with the prefrontal cortex and neocortex in the brain, as well as major nerve plexuses such as pelvic and gastric nerves.

From a psychological perspective, chakras have been compared with Maslow's hierarchy of needs, Erikson's stages of psychosocial development, Piaget's stages of cognitive development, and Freud's psychosexual stages.

Although these theories sound alluring, they do not adequately explain the holistic view taken by the eastern concept of chakras.

CONFLICTING OPINIONS ABOUT CHAKRAS

There are many conflicting opinions about the chakra system and its applications. Let's look at some of the common ideas that people are debating.

Chakras Don't Exist

Starting with the basics, many people deny the existence of chakras.

As discussed earlier, there is no tangible proof of their existence as yet, and ultimately, everyone should make up their own mind.

There Are Only Seven Chakras

The old yogic texts refer to many more than seven chakras. The system was simplified in the western traditions, and beginners are taught about a six-plus-one, or seven, chakra system.

Chakras Only Refer to Illnesses

New Age theories and treatments have reduced the usefulness of chakras to the healing of physical ailments.

According to the ancient Vedic texts, however, the main purpose of chakras is to elevate a person to a higher spiritual consciousness of the supreme divine presence in the universe.

It is Easy to Open the Chakras

Popular literature on the subject has portrayed chakras as simple energy centers that can be opened by emotional releases and yoga poses only.

The old texts paint a different picture, talking about significant shifts in consciousness and ways of thinking that have to occur. Many hours of meditation are necessary for the process to happen.

Balancing the Chakras Will Remove All Complaints

Physical and psychological complaints have physiological, emotional, and mental components that have to be addressed. Balancing the chakras cannot make problems vanish into thin air if the bases of the illnesses and discomforts have not been addressed.

You Cannot Control Your Chakras

Chakra balancing by practitioners of alternative therapies has become a popular and profitable business model. It is fueled by the myth that you are powerless to balance your own chakras.

If you set your mind to it, you can achieve anything. You can harness your willpower through the third chakra and take responsibility for your chakras.

Chakras Have to be Perfect

The state of our chakras change, just like our circumstances change. Chakras are flexible, and balancing becomes necessary when the situation demands it.

The Top Chakras are More Important

Thinking of the crown, brow, and throat chakras as more important than the lower ones is only one side of the coin. There needs to be a healthy interaction between the upper and lower chakras for the body and mind to be truly in balance and function optimally.

A Healer Needs Only One Session to Balance All the Chakras

Besides the point already made that balancing the chakras is not an instant process, it is also a myth to think that all responsibility can be shifted onto a healer to work miracles in one session.

We remain responsible for committing to being healed and working with the healing practitioner for as long as it takes, to achieve balance and true awareness.

2

THE ROOT CHAKRA—THE FOUNDATION

The image for the root chakra.

The root chakra is the foundation of the physical body. Balancing this chakra lays the foundation for balancing and opening the remaining six chakras.

In this chapter, we'll look at various methods of opening, balancing, and healing the root chakra, as well as discuss possible reasons why it could get blocked.

SUMMARY

Sanskrit name: Muladhara chakra
Color: Red
Seed mantra: Lam
Location: The base of the spine
Element: Earth
Gland: Adrenals
Psychological function: Basic survival, security, stability, and self-sufficiency

The Sanskrit Name

The word muladhara is a combination of the words 'mula,' meaning 'root,' and 'adhara,' which means 'base/support.'

The Color

Red is associated with the root chakra. It symbolizes strength and vitality, and links to our survival instincts and emotional needs for self-preservation.

The Seed Mantra

The seed mantra for the root chakra is 'lam.' That is the sound that produces the vibrations needed to bring us in contact with the primordial vibration of creation.

Location

It is located at the end of the tailbone, that is at the base of the spine, and between the genitals and anus.

Element

The root chakra is associated with the element of earth.

Gland

The muladhara chakra relates to the adrenal glands.

Psychological function

A balanced root chakra creates feelings of stability, groundedness, security, confidence, and energy.

UNDERSTANDING THE ROOT CHAKRA

The foundation of everything we are is enclosed in the root chakra. That includes our physical as well as all our energy bodies.

Sadhguru compares the significance of the root chakra with physical stability. Just as someone who does not feel steady on his legs won't climb a ladder, so we cannot climb the ladder of success and health without a confident grounding in the root chakra (2018).

The root chakra emanates a protective masculine energy that brings comfort and enables us to strive for the best in this world.

THE SPIRITUAL LAW GOVERNING THE ROOT CHAKRA

The law of karma governs the muladhara chakra. This law states that every action we perform while living on this earth will have a corresponding reaction.

The body can be used to make sure these reactions are allowing us to grow spiritually. The root chakra emanates signals about the possible effect of every decision we make, whether it will nourish our growth and meet our needs, or whether it will be toxic and put us back a step on our spiritual road. It is up to us to learn to listen to these signals. That can only happen if the root chakra is open and balanced.

Later in this chapter, we'll take a look at how that can be achieved.

WHAT CAN BLOCK THE ROOT CHAKRA?

Chakras get blocked from either too little or too much energy flow. They can be obstructed and slowed down, or get completely blocked.

Blockage of the root chakra can result from our modern way of thinking and living, which causes us to lose the connection to our true nature. The framework of modern society becomes our security network, and we try so hard to fit in that the opinion and approval of others become the guiding principle in our lives.

Our self-esteem plummets because we are constantly measuring ourselves against others. We also lose our authentic voices because we function from an overwhelming need to fit in with the beliefs of others.

That can bring stress, depression, anxiety, addictive behaviors, and lead to unhealthy relationships.

SIGNS OF AN UNBALANCED ROOT CHAKRA

A blocked root chakra will show itself in physical, as well as psychological signs.

Physically

Symptoms such as hypertension, lower back pain, impotence, indigestion, constipation, bladder problems, and unexplained body aches, especially in the legs and feet, may manifest themselves.

Psychologically

Depression, anxiety, insomnia, lethargy, a lack of motivation, feelings of isolation, restlessness, irritability, concentration problems, insecurity, codependency in relationships, and financial troubles can indicate problems with the root chakra.

RESTORING BALANCE AND HEALING THE ROOT CHAKRA

Provided you have the intention and commitment to open and balance your chakra, there are several things you can do to help you achieve that.

Use Red

The color red is associated with the muladhara chakra. Immerse yourself in the color by wearing it and using it in your decor and surroundings until you achieve balance again.

You can also use meditation. Visualize a bright sphere of red light, glowing at the end of the tailbone. See the red light in your mind's eye going down your legs, into your feet, and entering the ground to stabilize and ground you in the earth.

Recall this safe, stable feeling whenever your day gets hectic.

Move

Dancing is an excellent activity to balance the root chakra. Moving the legs and feet stimulates our connection to the earth and allows memories stored in our muscles to come free.

It doesn't matter how you move, or even if you can dance at all. The important thing is to move freely and as energetically as possible, like an animal would.

Close the door, shut the world out, and dance your root chakra open.

Eat From the Earth

Enjoy vegetables and fruit that grow in the earth to absorb the earth's energy.

Walk

Go for a walk in nature, even if it's in your own garden. Become aware of the sights and smells around you, and experience the different textures.

Concentrate on the feeling of your foot leaving the earth and then reconnecting when your foot comes down. Walk barefoot if at all possible.

Take a Shower

Water is naturally grounding, calming, and restoring. Getting rid of physical impurities in the shower can be a great aid in visualizing washing away everything that causes anxiety and stress too.

Look After Your Feet

Treating yourself to a pedicure is more than vanity. It can help to open and heal a blocked root chakra, as the feet are the contact points with the earth.

Stay Connected

Maintaining a strong connection with family and friends helps to keep the root chakra open and balanced. It promotes a feeling of security and "being at home."

Use Affirmations

Choose a couple of statements that reflect security and stability to use as affirmations. Write them down and stick the note where you will read it often.

Possible affirmations for the root chakra include:

- I am safe.
- I am loved as I am.
- I am enough.
- I am grounded.
- I have found my peace.
- I have self-love and I take care of myself because I am worth it.

Breathing Exercise

- Stand comfortably or sit in a position where your feet will still be flat on the ground.
- Relax your body and become still, turning your attention to your breathing.
- Imagine that you are exhaling right down to the soles of your feet and through your feet, so that your breath grows down like roots from your feet into the earth.
- On your inhalations, imagine pulling energy up from the earth, through your 'breath roots,' and through the soles of your feet into your pelvic region and the root chakra.
- Repeat the visualization for a couple of breaths and become

aware of how grounded your legs and hips feel.

Yoga

Practice these asanas, or poses, to help with balancing the root chakra:

Shavasana/Corpse Pose

Although shavasana is often done at the end of a yoga session to relax, it can be performed at any time. It is an easy pose, suitable for any level.

- Lie on your back with your legs straight and relaxed—allow your feet to fall to the sides.
- Position a folded blanket over your thighs to emphasize the feeling of being grounded and connected to the earth.
- Keep your arms to your sides and slightly away from your body.
- Hold your hands with the palms facing upward; relax your fingers and allow them to curl upward.
- Tuck your shoulder blades toward the back.
- Relax your whole body now, including your face.
- Breathe naturally and comfortably.
- Keep the pose for five to 10 minutes. Set an alarm so you can relax completely and don't have to keep checking the time.
- When you feel ready, wiggle your fingers and toes, and stretch your whole body.
- Bring your knees up to your chest and roll onto your side, into a fetal position.
- Stay in the fetal position with your eyes closed for a few

moments, savoring the safe, relaxed feeling in your body.
- Push yourself up into a sitting position and open your eyes.

Surya Namaskara/ Sun Salutations

The sun salutations consist of a sequence of 12 poses, performed twice.

- Start in a standing position with your feet together and your weight balanced equally on both feet (prayer pose).
- Keep your shoulders relaxed but your body upright, so that your chest is expanded.
- Breathe in while lifting your arms.
- Breathe out while joining your palms together in front of your chest in a prayer position.
- Breathe in again and lift your arms up and toward the back, keeping the upper arms close to the ears. The goal of this pose is to stretch the whole body, from toe to finger tips (raised arms pose).
- Breathe out while bending forward at the waist; place your hands on the floor beside your feet if you can—bend your knees if you need to (standing forward bend).
- Now, stretch your left leg out behind you and lower your left knee toward the floor, while looking up and breathing in again (equestrian pose).
- Stretch your right leg out behind you too, to bring the body into a straight line (stick pose).
- Lower both knees to the ground while breathing out.
- Lower your chest and chin to the floor too; push your

posterior upward slightly to achieve this. Both hands, both knees, both feet, your chest, and your chin should touch the floor (salute with eight points).
- Slide forward to straighten your body and lift your chest in the pose of a cobra, ready to strike. Keep your elbows bent and look up toward the ceiling (cobra pose).
- Breathe out while lifting the hips and posterior up to put the body into an inverted 'V' shape (downward facing dog pose).
- Slide the right foot forward between the hands, with your left knee on the floor. Press your hips down and look up toward the ceiling (equestrian pose).
- Bring the left foot forward too while breathing out, with the palms remaining on the floor. Bend your knees if necessary (standing forward bend).
- Roll your spine into a standing position, raise your arms, and stretch them to the back while looking up (raised arms pose).
- Exhale while straightening your body and lowering your arms (mountain pose).
- Relax in this position for a moment before repeating the sequence, this time starting with your right foot and leg in the equestrian pose.

Shashankasana/Hare's Pose and Balasama/Child's Pose

Both these poses are used to rest the body and calm the mind.

- Sit in a kneeling position with your knees hip-width apart.
- Lower your torso to your thighs.
- Your buttocks should touch your heels; if you find that too

difficult, you can put a rolled up blanket or towel over your calves.
- For the hare's pose, stretch your arms forward on the floor with your palms facing down and your shoulders relaxed.
- For the child's pose, stretch your arms to the back with your palms facing upward, like a baby would sleep.

Ardha Setu Bandhasana/Half Bridge Pose

This is an asana that stretches the lower back and lumbar area.

- Lie down on your back with your knees bent and your feet close to your hips. Keep your feet hip-width apart and your heels flat on the floor.
- Place your hands by your sides with your palms facing downward.
- Push your hands down while breathing in and slowly push your hips up.
- Slide your hands forward and lift your chest toward your chin.
- Hold the position for a few moments before lowering your hips in a controlled manner, vertebra by vertebra.

Sukha Hanumanasana/Easy Monkey Pose

The proper monkey pose is a full split that can be difficult for beginners in yoga to do. This variation still provides a good stretch for the hamstrings, which are connected to our fight-or-flight response.

- Start in the downward facing dog pose, as discussed in the sun salutations.
- Move your right foot gradually forward, toward your right thumb.
- Drop your left knee down to the floor.
- Pull your hips back to be positioned above your left knee and straighten your right leg, keeping your right foot flexed.
- If you find it difficult to keep your hands on the ground, support them on yoga blocks.

Malasana/Garland Pose

The garland pose activates the soles of the feet, which sensitizes us to our connection with the earth. It is a deep squat that opens up the hips and groin.

- Stand on a yoga mat with your feet the width of the mat apart. If you have difficulty balancing or your muscles are very tight, start with your back against a wall for support.
- Bend your knees and lower your body into a squatting position, keeping your feet flat on the floor. If you find that difficult, place a rolled-up towel under your heels to keep the pressure of the pose backward instead of forward. Your hips have to stay lower too, otherwise the pressure will always be focused forward instead of backward. Sit on a yoga block or two if dropping your hips is a problem for you.
- Allow your toes to turn out, but not too much. Work on keeping them as close as parallel to each other as possible.
- Bring your upper arms to the inside of your knees, bend your

elbows, and join your palms in the prayer position.
- Bend your thumbs backward to touch your sternum if you can, but don't force anything.
- Keep your spine straight.
- Stay in the position for five breathing cycles (one inhalation and one exhalation) before straightening the legs and returning to an upright position.

Uttanasana/Standing Forward Bend

This powerful pose is much more than touching your toes. It is about stretching the entire back body that starts at the soles of the feet and ends between the eyes, having gone all the way up the back of the legs, back, and head.

Warming up before attempting uttanasana is a good idea, especially if your muscles and tendons are stiff.

When done successfully, the standing forward bend relieves anxiety, calms the mind, and aids digestion.

The pose has been discussed briefly in the sun salutations, but let's look at starting from effective warm-ups to attain the pose safely.

- The cat-cow pose is useful to learn what it feels like to tilt and tuck the pelvis to obtain full stretches.
- Start on your hands and knees with your wrists positioned directly beneath your shoulders, and your knees directly beneath your hips.

- Take a deep, relaxed breath and tilt your tailbone up to create an arc. That is the tilted pelvis of the cow pose.
- Breathe out and reverse the movement by dropping the pelvis and drawing your abdominals toward your spine to create a rounded back. That is the feeling of the tucked pelvis of the cat pose.
- Repeat this sequence eight to 10 times.
- Move from this pose into the downward facing dog position, which looks like an inverted 'V' (see the sun salutations).
- Now move into uttasana by standing upright in the mountain pose with some form of restraint like a yoga block on the outside of each foot.
- With your palms flat against the top of your thighs, bend forward at the waist with the same pelvis tilting movement you experienced in the cow pose.
- Bend forward as far as you can—if you feel any strain in your hamstrings, lower back, or neck, bend your knees.
- Drop your head down and relax your neck.
- Stay in the pose for five breathing cycles.

Virabhadrasana II/Warrior II

This pose is named after a fierce warrior, Virabhadra, who is said to have been an incarnation of the god Shiva.

The pose keeps both feet planted firmly on the ground to strengthen stamina and inner power.

- Start in the mountain pose (see the sun salutations).

- Breathe in and on the exhalation, step or jump your feet three and a half to four feet apart from each other.
- Raise your arms parallel to the floor with your palms facing down and your shoulder blades open.
- Turn your right foot slightly to the right and align your left and right heels.
- Turn your left thigh outward enough to align the center of your left knee cap to the center of your left ankle.
- On an exhalation, bend your left knee over your left ankle to position the shin perpendicular to the floor.
- Press your outer right heel firmly down to the floor.
- Keep your shoulders positioned over your pelvis and pull your tailbone slightly toward your pubis.
- Turn your head to the left and look out over your left fingers.
- Stay in the pose for 30 seconds to one minute before coming upright and reversing the position.

Vrikshasana/Tree Pose

The tree pose is one of the few standing positions in yoga. It improves balance and tones the feet, inner thighs, groin, and hips.

It is also an easy beginner pose. Be patient with yourself if you wobble or fall over in the beginning. Remember, this exercise is about loving and accepting you for who you are. You are safe.

- Start in the mountain pose and become aware of your weight being equally distributed on your feet.

- Shift your weight gradually onto your right foot and lift your left foot off the floor. Keep your right leg straight without locking your knee. Keep your hands in the prayer position.
- Bend your left knee and lift your left foot as high as possible against your right inner thigh. Don't put your foot against your knee, to avoid injury and unnecessary pressure on the knee joint. If your foot can't reach above your knee, rather press against your calf.
- Keep your hips squared, don't allow your right hip to jut out. It will be easier if you press your left foot and your right thigh equally hard against each other.
- Concentrate on keeping your left knee turned out, away from the center line, to feel the stretch.
- Focus your gaze in front of you, on something that does not move. When you feel comfortable in the pose, you can try closing your eyes to see if you can still keep your balance.
- Keep the tree pose for five to 10 breathing cycles before lowering your left foot and reversing the pose.
- When you feel confident enough in your balance, you can stretch your arms up to the ceiling in either a straight line or a V-shape.
- You can also try lifting your left foot higher, positioning it in the crease of your right hip in a half-lotus position.

Tadasana/Mountain Pose

The mountain pose strengthens the spine and improves the general posture. It is a foundation for many other poses.

Although this pose looks like you're just standing, it is more than that. It requires awareness of body alignment while it strengthens the spine and legs.

- Stand with your feet close enough to each other that your big toes are touching. If you feel unstable in this position, keep your feet hip-wide first until you are more comfortable.
- Lift all your toes and put them slightly fanned down again to create a stable base for standing.
- Draw the muscles on the front of your thighs up until you feel your knee caps rise.
- Turn your thighs inward to widen the pelvis bone area.
- Keep your spine straight but natural.
- Drop your shoulders and make sure they are positioned over your pelvis.
- Pull your shoulders now up to your ears and hold them for a moment before rolling them back to release your shoulder blades.
- Let your arms hang down naturally with your elbows slightly bent and your palms facing forward.
- Become aware that your neck is long and your crown is reaching toward the ceiling.
- Do five to 10 breathing cycles while holding this position.

Muladhara Mudra/Root-Supporting Mudra

A mudra is a symbolic hand gesture that is used to improve concentration and assist in the flow of energy and healing.

- Sit upright in a comfortable position.
- Lift your hands toward your heart and bring your palms together in a prayer position.
- Interlace your pinkies and ring fingers and fold them inside your palms.
- Extend your middle fingers.
- Interlace your index fingers and thumbs to form rings around each other. The fingertips should be touching.
- You can also lower your arms slightly and turn the mudra upside down, so your outstretched middle fingers point at your pelvic region.

Gemstones and Crystals

Several stones and crystals resonate with the muladhara chakra.

Red Jasper

As a gemstone with the same color as the root chakra, red jasper is a strong and powerful reminder of personal strength and endurance.

It emanates a grounding energy that helps you to stay connected to your spiritual power.

Red Aventurine

Emotionally, red aventurine aids in releasing stored trauma to strengthen the connection to Source energy. On the physical side, the stone helps to detoxify and purify the body, promoting better blood flow.

Bloodstone

Bloodstone is an interesting gemstone that combines the colors red and green.

Red speaks of its cleansing and healing properties, while the dark green relates to new growth, fearlessness, and protection against negativity.

The stone was known as heliotrope in ancient Greece, and the name is still used sometimes today.

Black Tourmaline

Black tourmaline has been used since ancient times as protection against negativity and spiritual attacks. It provides grounding energy for the base chakra.

Smokey Quartz

The smokey quartz family comes in various shades of brown and grey, from light to dark.

It helps to dissolve emotional blockages caused by an imbalance in the root chakra. It restores calm and puts material events and possessions into perspective.

Carnelian

This is a brilliant orange-red stone to boost self-confidence and willpower. It also fuels passion and creativity from a strengthened connection to Source.

Hematite

This shiny black gemstone draws negativity from your aura and filters it out through the root chakra, leaving you less anxious and more grounded.

It also aids logical, clear thinking and helps you keep at a distance from other people's drama.

Jet

Jet is a mineral that is formed out of fossilized wood. It absorbs negativity and brings back balance.

Garnet

Garnet is a regenerative stone that can energize low energy levels without overstimulating them.

It also promotes emotional energy by increasing courage and strengthening the survival instinct.

Poppy Jasper

This mottled red gemstone can restore serenity and calm to a root chakra that is overstimulated.

It can also boost self-confidence when you get in contact with demanding people, providing the courage to establish personal boundaries.

The stone emanates a warm, compassionate energy that stimulates joy and optimism.

Onyx

The beautiful black onyx is credited with sharpening physical responses and boosting the senses, which makes it perfect for the root chakra that is associated with our physical well-being.

Essential Oils and Herbs

Vetiver, myrrh, turmeric, patchouli, ginger, frankincense, cedarwood, spruce, sandalwood, palo santo, ylang ylang, geranium, black pepper, rose, lavender, burdock, clove, dandelion, rosemary, paprika, nutmeg, and cypress are all grounding, centering, and calming. That clears the mind, so you can get in touch with your real nature once again.

Foods

The foods that can aid in balancing the root chakra are red-colored fruits and vegetables, root vegetables, as well as protein from plant sources, to help the connection to the earth.

Good vegan sources of protein include tofu, edamame, lentils, black beans, amaranth, quinoa, black-eyed peas, hemp, pumpkin, and chia seeds, spinach, green peas, broccoli, almonds, spirulina, chickpeas, tahini, peanut butter, hemp and soy milk, and tempeh.

Healthy root vegetable choices include sweet potato, parsnips, onion, garlic, carrots, beets, and rutabaga.

Affirmations

Repeating phrases that help you open your root chakra during meditation, or whenever you feel like during the day, can reinforce the grounded, safe energy you are seeking to unblock.

Here are a few suggestions for affirmations to get you started.

- My root chakra is open.
- My root chakra is balanced.
- I feel protected in my world.
- I am safe.
- I am grounded and centered.
- Everything is well in my world.
- I choose to trust the guidance of the universe.
- I choose to trust there is good in the world.
- I am deeply connected to my body.
- I am everything I need for my happiness.

A Guided Meditation

Meditation frees the mind from the incessant inner chatter and negative remarks we direct to ourselves. Use the following guided meditation to balance and heal your root chakra.

Hold the root chakra gemstones or crystals while you meditate, or arrange them around you. Build yourself a mandala by placing gemstones, herbs, and spices around or near you to enhance the effect of your meditation.

Record the script for this meditation on your cell phone to make meditating easy. Just remember to read slowly and give yourself enough time to move from step to step.

Find a comfortable position in a favorite chair, on a yoga mat, or a bed.

Fold your hands loosely in your lap and keep your feet relaxed on the floor if you are sitting.

If you are lying down, keep your legs straight and don't cross your ankles. Keep your arms next to your body on the bed or fold your hands over your midsection.

Place a pillow under your knees if you need it for comfort—your aim is loving yourself and allowing yourself space to be the glorious being you are.

Close your eyes and become aware of all the surfaces touching you. Are they warm, soft, smooth, or coarse? Notice their support.

Breathe in deeply and let the air fill your abdomen and your chest. Feel the air moving into your lungs and expand your chest.

When you exhale, send the energizing air down into your root chakra and feel it relax and open.

Breathe in...and out.

And in...and out.

And again, breathe in...and out.

And in...and out.

Focus your attention on your root chakra. Know that you are home and safe, you can rest here. You don't need anything outside of that.

Imagine yourself curling up in the embrace of your root

chakra like a small child in the lap of a parent. Remind yourself that all is well.

Feel the warmth of all the love there is for you and know you are worth that love. Know too that you have no beginning and no end and you are truly wonderful. You are precious and unique.

Breathe in...and out.

And in...and out.

And again, breathe in...and out.

And in...and out.

Become aware of being in perfect balance, grounded in the energy of the earth and the feeling of being safe, whatever the circumstances.

Hold a warm feeling of acceptance and caring for yourself inside and allow it to expand and fill you with warmth as far as it will go. Do not force anything, just let it move. Savor this warmth.

[Pause]

When you feel ready, stir your arms and legs and slowly become aware of the sounds of the outside world again.

Open your eyes.

Music

The right music can be a great help to balance the root chakra. There are many recordings of traditional music available online.

Music specifically composed for balancing the root chakra can be accessed freely at several places online. These include:

- https://www.youtube.com/watch?v=7Xhof7mETqI
- https://www.youtube.com/watch?v=GqgN3yec0Gk

Contemporary music should be in the key of C major to affect the root chakra. Examples of such songs include "Let it Be," by The Beatles, "I Will Survive," by Gloria Gaynor, "No Woman No Cry," by Bob Marley, "Piano Man," by Billy Joel, "Ain't No Mountain High Enough," by Diana Ross, "Holding Back the Years," by Simply Red, "Buon Natale (Means Merry Christmas to You)," by Nat King Cole, "(I've Been) Searchin' So Long," by Chicago, "Only the Good Die Young," by Billy Joel, and "Daniel," by Elton John.

Other Activities

Sometimes, the small things can make a huge impact. Anything that will make you feel more loved, grounded, and secure can help your root chakra on the road to balance and health.

Treat yourself to luxurious new bedding, do a deep-clean of your home, and set up a sacred corner in your living space where you keep items that are significant for you to feel safe and appreciated.

3

THE SACRAL CHAKRA—WHERE THE SELF DWELLS

The image for the sacral chakra.

SUMMARY

Sanskrit name: Svadhisthana chakra
Color: Orange

Seed mantra: Vam

Location: Lower abdomen

Element: Water

Gland: Gonads

Psychological function: Sexuality, desires, creativity, and self-worth

THE SANSKRIT NAME

The Sanskrit word svadhisthana means "the dwelling place of the self." It consists of the words 'swa,' meaning 'self,' and 'adhisthana,' meaning 'seat' or 'basis.'

The Color

Orange is the color associated with the sacral chakra. It is reminiscent of sunrise and symbolizes the rise of personal consciousness out of darkness.

The Seed Mantra

The seed mantra for the sacral chakra is 'vam.'

Location

The sacral chakra is located at the hips and sexual organs, about four fingers below the navel.

Element

The sacral chakra is associated with the element of water and its powerful flow of creativity, as well as its potential for destroying when it is not properly regulated.

Gland

The sacral chakra influences the gonads, that are the ovaries in women and the testicles in men. It also relates to the bladder, kidneys, and prostate.

Psychological function

A balanced sacral chakra creates feelings of fulfillment and contentment in sexual and intimate relationships. Creativity in all aspects of life flow freely.

UNDERSTANDING THE SACRAL CHAKRA

The second chakra is the seat of creativity, sexuality, and personal expansion. When it is balanced and spinning as it should, you will feel empowered emotionally to forge relationships with intimate partners, as well as friends and family close to you.

You will be open to the creation and birth of new projects, new pastimes, and, in a physical sense, a child. A blocked sacral chakra is often associated with physical infertility.

It will be easier to find solutions to problems when your vitality flows freely through your center of creativity.

THE SPIRITUAL LAW GOVERNING THE SACRAL CHAKRA

The spiritual law of Least Effort governs the second chakra. It teaches that we co-create our lives when we start from a creative point.

That means living and creating in joy, harmony, and with a carefree attitude.

The foundation for this law comes from nature. Plants don't force their growth and put in a huge effort, they just do it. Flowers bloom, fish swim, and birds fly because that is their essence.

It is an essential part of our human experience to manifest our dreams and ideals into physical form. That should be just as natural to us as growing is to a plant. Opening and balancing the sacral chakra is the first step toward reclaiming that ability.

The motivation for manifesting the most while expending the least effort should be love (Chopra, 2020).

WHAT CAN BLOCK THE SACRAL CHAKRA?

Any illness of the reproductive system or urinary tract, sexual trauma, chronic stress, and emotional issues regarding creativity can cause the sacral chakra to get blocked or out of balance.

SIGNS OF AN UNBALANCED SACRAL CHAKRA

The symptoms include the following:

Physically

Frigidity or impotence, gynaecological problems, premenstrual syndrome and other period-related problems, prostatitis, urinary tract infections, lower back pain, arthritis, problems with the hip joint, kidney issues, weight gain that stubbornly refuses to budge.

Psychologically

An inability to experience pleasure through the senses, loss of interest in sexual activities, an aversion to intimacy in any interpersonal relationships, not only sexual; loss of interest in creative pastimes and difficulty creating, such as struggling with writer's block or sudden stage fright; addictive behaviors that can include food, leading to unwanted weight gain; mood swings and untamed outbursts of emotion; sustained high levels of stress and the release of stress hormones such as cortisol.

RESTORING BALANCE AND HEALING THE SACRAL CHAKRA

Let's look at some activities to balance your sacral chakra.

The Water Connection

Any type of water, flowing or still, will speak to the sacral chakra because it is associated with the element of water.

Spending time at the ocean or a river, whether you are swimming or just sitting, will be just as beneficial as taking a long, warm bath to stabilize your emotional center.

Just drinking water will also aid the healing of the sacral chakra.

Orange

Use the color orange wherever you can. Wear it, use it in your home decor, and eat orange foods.

Dance

Any type of dance that gets your hips moving is great for the second chakra. Think belly dancing and Hawaii-style swaying movements.

The tempo of the dance does not matter—it can be sensuously slow, or fast and erotic.

Stillness

Take a few minutes every day out of your hectic schedule to sit quietly and be mindful. What do you see, what do you hear, what do you smell, what do you feel?

Getting in touch with yourself and your mind will help heal your emotions and intimate relationships with others.

Experience Your Qi

As the sacral chakra is all about creating, a visualization exercise to experience your qi, or life force, works well to heal this chakra. This exercise allows your emotions to create your experience instead of trying to rationalize qi with the logical mind.

Hold your hands in front of you with your palms facing each other. It is the prayer position but without the hands touching. Keep your hands about two inches apart.

Look at the space between your palms and allow your hands to drift apart slowly. Feel the tingling sensation of energy building between your hands.

Move them closer again and create a vibrant orange ball of energy in your mind's eye.

Imagine the ball to be pliable and, as you move your hands apart again, see the ball growing. When you bring your hands back closer together again, see the ball getting smaller. Breathe in the light, warmth, and peace of the energy ball.

You can also visualize the ball of energy to be pulsing, sending its energy to you to inhale and incorporate into your body.

Keep a Journal

Writing in a journal, or keeping a scrapbook if you are more visually inclined, is another great way to stay in touch with your feelings and emotions.

Give structure to your writing by asking yourself some questions first:

- Am I happy with my sex life?
- Is my lifestyle fueling my creative passions?

- What does being empowered in my sexual experiences look like to me?
- Why am I afraid of getting close to people?

Breathing Exercise

- Make abdominal breathing a part of your daily life.
- Whenever you have a few minutes to concentrate on breathwork, become aware of your breathing.
- Straighten your torso and lift your ribcage, whether you are sitting or standing.
- Relax your shoulders and breathe in as deeply as possible without lifting them again.
- While you inhale, allow your abdominal wall and stomach to expand with air.
- Visualize the air swirling around the disc of your sacral chakra, animating and feeding it with energy.
- When you exhale, contract your abdomen toward your spine.
- Feel the heat generated in your lower body by the activated energy.

Yoga

Practice these asanas, or poses, to help with balancing the sacral chakra:

Baddha Konasana/Butterfly Pose

This restorative stretch opens up the hips and stretches the hip flexors.

- Sit down on the floor or a yoga mat and put the soles of your feet together.
- Hold your ankles with your hands.
- Gently press your knees down as far as is comfortable for you; do not force any movement.
- Keep your spine long and straight.
- Fold your upper body down over your legs as far as it can go without rounding your back.
- If sitting in this position is too difficult, you can modify the stretch by sitting on a chair.
- Put one foot on the opposite knee to form a figure four and gently push your bent knee down while hinging forward from the hips.
- Keep your back straight.
- Remember to do the other leg as well.

Kakasana/Crow Pose

The crow pose turns your arms into the legs of the bird, your hands into its feet, and your folded-up body becomes the crow's body. The secret of this pose lies in learning to get the weight of the upper and lower body in counterbalance against each other.

It is not a beginner's pose and care should be taken to warm up properly and not attempt movements your body is not ready for yet.

- Prepare by starting in a forward fold (your body bent forward, over your legs, from the waist) and keep your feet the distance of your inner hips apart.
- Bend your knees as deeply as you need to press your palms flat on the floor or yoga mat. You can start with blocks under your hands if reaching the floor is too difficult in the beginning.
- Round your back while pressing your hands down to stretch the trapezius muscles between the shoulder blades.
- Next, stretch your hip muscles by going into a deep squat.
- Keep your feet as wide as your yoga mat and turn your toes out.
- Sink your hips down between your heels as far as they can go.
- Hold your elbows inside your knees and fold your hands over your heart in the prayer position.
- Support your backside with blocks if you experience any pain in your hips or knees.

Doing the Crow

- Enter into another forward bend, but keep your heels together this time and your toes apart.
- Bend your knees and press your hands down firmly on the ground beneath your shoulders.
- Bending your elbows back, raise your heels from the ground. Your toes will still be touching the floor.

- Pull your knees into your armpits and allow your shins to rest on your triceps.
- Slowly tilt the weight of your body forward and keep your gaze about two inches before you.
- Round your upper back.
- Engage your core and lift first one foot off the ground and then the other.

Trikonasana/Triangle Pose

The triangle pose is an easy position, accessible to any beginner. It strengthens the groin, hips, and hamstrings while stretching and opening the chest and loosening the shoulders.

- Start in a standing position with your feet three and a half to four feet apart.
- Turn your left foot out about 15 degrees and turn your right foot to a 90 degree angle.
- Check that the center of your right heel aligns to the center of the arch of your left foot.
- Balance your weight equally on both feet.
- Breathe in deeply, and on the exhalation, bend your body to the right from your hips.
- Keep your waist straight.
- Reach your right hand down toward the floor while allowing your left hand to stretch up to the sky. Keep your arms in a straight line with each other.
- Let your right hand rest on your shin or lower—choose the lowest spot you can manage without folding your waist.

- Turn your head to the left or keep it in a neutral position, whatever feels most comfortable to you.
- Make sure your body is in a straight line and not tilted backward or forward. If you don't have a mirror close by, ask someone to correct your alignment until you know what it should feel like.
- Stretch to the maximum limit you can on every exhalation.
- Repeat the stretch on the other side.

Dvipada Pitham/Activated Bridge Pose

The activated bridge pose is a dynamic exercise that requires movement from you, while the passive bridge pose variation requires no movement. Both of these exercises strengthen and stretch the hips, lower back, spine, and chest.

The passive bridge pose is called setu bandhasana and the arms are kept next to the body while the hips are lifted, instead of stretched out behind the head. The position is assumed and held.

- Lie on your back with your feet flat on the floor or your yoga mat.
- Inhale and lift your arms up and over your head, while simultaneously lifting your hips up so your torso is in a straight line.
- Lower your arms and hips on the exhalation in a controlled movement and feel every vertebra pressing back onto the floor or mat.
- Repeat the exercise five times.

Salamba Bhujangasana/Sphinx Pose

The sphinx pose is a great stretch for the spine. It can be used by beginners as an introduction to the cobra pose (bhujangasana) or on its own.

It is beneficial for anyone with lower back problems because it causes less pressure on the spine than the cobra pose.

- Start by lying face down on a yoga mat or the floor. Keep your toes flat against the floor and your forehead touching the ground.
- Your feet and heels should be touching each other lightly.
- Stretch your arms flat on the ground in front of you with your palms facing downward.
- Breathe in deeply while gently lifting your head and chest off the ground. Support your weight on your forearms and hands.
- Keep breathing deeply and evenly while you imagine your tailbone lengthening and shifting down to curl around your lower back, protecting it.
- Hold the position for five to 10 breaths.
- On an exhalation, gently lower your head and chest back down to the floor.

Jathara Parivrtti/Supine Spinal Twist-A

The spinal twist, also known as a belly twist, lengthens and stretches the back muscles and helps to realign the spine.

- Lie on your back with your knees bent and your feet flat on the floor or yoga mat.
- Keep your arms outstretched to the sides, palms facing upward.
- Move your hips slightly to your right side and allow your knees to fall to your left side, twisting your spine and lower back.
- Slide your knees up to as close to your left arm as possible, while looking at your right finger tips.
- Make sure your shoulders stay flat on the floor.
- Relax your body and allow gravity to do the work.
- Hold the position for five to 10 breaths.
- Roll back to the center on an exhalation and repeat the twist to the other side.

Kapotasana/Pigeon Pose

The pigeon pose provides a great stretch for the hips and lower back, bringing back flexibility to hip flexors that can get tight from too much sitting.

- This position starts from the downward dog. See the sun salutations explained in the chapter about the root chakra.
- From the upside down V-shape of the downward dog, raise your right leg to touch your right knee to the back of your right wrist.
- Turn your right shin to be parallel to the front of your yoga mat.
- Keep your left leg straight.

- Make sure your right knee is further to the right than your right hip.
- Flex your right foot toward your shin and lower your right thigh gently. If this is difficult for you to do without straining, you can place a folded towel under your thigh.
- Position your hands under your shoulders and press on your hands to push your spine upright.
- Puff out your chest, keep your gaze forward, and feel your spine stretch.
- Slowly lower your upper body to the ground as far as you can go and keep the position for 10 breaths.
- Repeat the pose for the other side.

Supta Baddha Konasana/Goddess Pose

Prevent or relieve back pain and sciatica with this excellent stretch for the groin and hips.

- Lie down on your back, bend your knees, and place the soles of your feet together.
- Let your knees fall down and do not arch your lower back. If you find that impossible, support your lower back with a folded towel.
- Allow gravity to deepen the stretch and stay in the position for as long as is comfortable while breathing deeply and evenly.

Dhanurasana/Bow Pose

In this pose, the body looks like the bow of an archer. It is an intermediate pose that strengthens the abdominal muscles and back. It is also believed to stimulate the reproductive organs and improve period-related problems.

- Lie on your stomach on a yoga mat.
- Reach behind you and take hold of your outer ankles.
- On an exhalation, lift your upper body to form the shape of a bow.
- Try to rest your weight on your lower abdomen, rather than on your hips or ribs.
- Pull back on your feet if you can do it without hurting yourself and lift yourself even higher.
- Hold the position for three breaths before releasing.
- Repeat the pose.

Shakti Mudra/Empowerment Mudra

This mudra is associated with enhancing sensuality and sexuality for both sexes, although the energy of the mudra is feminine.

- Sit comfortably and hold your palms together in front of your chest.
- Press the tips of your ring fingers and pinkies together.
- Fold your thumbs to the insides of your palms.
- Press the knuckles of your index and middle fingers together

or keep them separate, if the position is more comfortable for you.
- Lower your hands to below your navel.

Gemstones and Crystals

Several stones and crystals resonate with the sacral chakra.

This beautiful reddish orange gemstone was revered by ancient civilizations as a fertility enhancer and was strongly associated with the goddess of fertility, Aphrodite/Isis.

It is seen as a stone for stimulating creativity, leadership, endurance, passion, intuition, and confidence.

Orange Calcite

Orange calcite is used to move negative energy out and allow creativity and motivation in. It gently opens the sacral chakra to encourage you to see the truth in things, break bad habits, and live up to your full potential.

Tiger's Eye

Balance your gateway for the creative force of life, which is the second chakra, with the aid of the beautiful tiger's eye gemstone.

It can balance yin and yang and stabilize fluctuating emotions.

When creativity flows freely again, confidence, intuition, and self-knowledge all get a boost too.

Tiger's eye is also used to stimulate kundalini energy.

Amber

Although amber is not strictly speaking a crystal because it is fossilized tree resin, it is still a powerful aid to open and balance the sacral chakra.

It contains fauna and flora from ancient times in which energies that transcend time are stored and can help you clear emotional blockages to reconnect with your intuition.

It boosts decisiveness, spontaneity, and confidence—also in sexual matters.

Orange Moonstone

This crystal is one of the best to restore emotional balance and relieve anxiety.

Its association with the lunar cycles makes it a particularly helpful stone for women. It is used as a talisman for relationships and fertility.

If your self-love is suffering because of body issues and eating disorders, orange moonstone can help you separate emotional reasons for eating from the physical need for food.

Sunstone

Sunstone boosts leadership, motivation, confidence, and personal power. It can help you to take charge of your emotions and relationships with a light and joyful energy.

Let your true, kind, and vibrant personality shine through with the help of the sunstone.

Goldstone

Known as the stone of ambition, goldstone is an excellent choice to ground you in healing spiritual power to unlock your full personal potential.

Although it is a manmade stone, goldstone has powerful properties derived from the copper and glass it is made up of.

It also has a calming effect on troubled emotions, clearing the stage for a sustained focus on creativity.

Aragonite Star Clusters

These intricate and delicate crystal clusters not only turn the mind to healing and nurturing the self, but also to conservation of the planet.

It resonates with creativity and self-sustainability and helps us to achieve a renewed sense of balance.

It can assist in cancelling the frustration, anger, and stress caused by a work-life balance that got out of whack.

The cluster formation radiates the stone's energy, which makes it excellent for shielding against negative energy coming from others.

Tangerine Quartz

All quartz are powerful crystals, but the tangerine version is outstanding for balancing the sacral chakra.

It encourages a playful curiosity about life to boost self-knowledge and acceptance and enhance creativity. It brings the *joie d'vivre* back, energizing your love and sexual life.

Orange/Imperial Topaz

The reddish-orange variety of the normally transparent topaz is one of the rarest and most sought-after crystals. It is sometimes also called golden topaz, although golden mostly refers to the stones with a more yellow hue.

Orange topaz can enhance self-confidence and banish negative feelings. It can boost feelings of self-worth and confidence and help you to attract the right people.

Essential Oils and Herbs

Lavender, patchouli, ylang ylang, tangerine, rose, helichrysum, sweet orange, pink pepper seed, coconut, ginger, vanilla, fennel, and cinnamon are all recommended for healing the sacral chakra.

Foods

The key for the sacral chakra is all things orange. Carrots, pumpkin, butternut, mango, yellow bell peppers, peaches, apricots, sweet potatoes, nectarines, persimmons, and oranges are all on the menu.

Moist foods containing lots of seeds such as passion fruit and strawberry also work well.

Foods rich in omega-3 oils such as salmon, sardines, tuna, and mackerel will also be beneficial. Add some nuts and seeds such as almonds, flax, sesame, and walnuts.

Affirmations

Here are a few suggestions for affirmations to get you started.

- My sacral chakra is open.
- My sacral chakra is balanced.
- I attract the right people who respect me and my boundaries.
- I find pleasure in all areas of my life.
- My emotions flow freely.
- I am vibrantly sensual.
- I embrace my sexuality.
- I nourish my soul by creating art.
- I welcome my intuitive senses.
- I honor and enjoy my body.

A Guided Meditation

Use the following guided meditation to balance and heal your sacral chakra.

Hold the gemstones or crystals for the sacral chakra while you meditate, or arrange them around you. Build yourself a mandala by placing gemstones, herbs, and spices around or near you to enhance the effect of your meditation.

Record the script for this meditation on your cell phone to make meditating easy. Just remember to read slowly and give yourself enough time to move from step to step.

> *Find a comfortable position in a favorite chair, on a yoga mat, or a bed.*
> *Fold your hands loosely in your lap and keep your feet relaxed on the floor if you are sitting.*
> *If you are lying down, keep your legs straight and don't cross your ankles. Keep your arms next to your body on the bed or fold your hands over your midsection.*
> *Place a pillow under your knees if you need it for comfort.*
> *Close your eyes and imagine the earth opening its arms to fold you safely in its embrace.*
> *Be aware of the infinite love there is for you and breathe it in with every deep...calm...breath.*
> *Breathe out all feelings of loneliness and rejection...and breathe love in...and negativity out.*
> *Feel a deep joy starting to bubble within you because you are free and loved and supported.*
> *Visualize the joy as an vibrant orange glow below your navel, filling you with warmth and love.*
> *Watch the glow spread all over your body, bathing you in joy.*
> *Breathe in pure joy...and exhale all sadness.*
> *Savor the joy for as long as you like.*
> *[Pause]*
> *When you feel ready, stir your arms and legs and slowly become aware of the sounds of the outside world again. Open your eyes.*

Music

Music specifically composed for balancing the sacral chakra can be accessed freely at several places online. These include:

- https://www.youtube.com/watch?v=YxnKBMblrXk
- https://www.youtube.com/watch?v=NDAw99HazUE

Besides traditional music that is available online, any contemporary music in the key of D will resonate with the sacral chakra. Examples include "Waterloo," by Abba, "Under Pressure," by Queen, "Blowin' in the Wind," by Bob Dylan, "Always On My Mind," by Willie Nelson, "Scarborough Fair," by Simon and Garfunkel, "Strong Enough," by Sheryl Crowe, "Fields of Gold," by Sting, "Harvest Moon," by Neil Young, "Tougher Than the Rest," by Bruce Springsteen, and "Maybe I'm Amazed," by Paul McCartney.

Other Activities

A moving meditation can work wonders for the sacral chakra. It means performing movements while focusing on your breathing at the same time.

Here is one for you to try:

> Start from a position on your hands and knees on a yoga mat or blanket.
> Inhale deeply through your nose. On the exhalation, drop your head down to your chest and lower your tailbone. Round your back and feel your spine stretch.

On the next inhalation, lift your tailbone back up while dropping your belly toward the floor. Lift your heart to face forward.

Do this cycle a few times and focus on combining your breath with every movement.

Next, drop your hips back toward your heels and reach your arms straight out in front of you. Start making circles with your hips, first circling to the right, then forward, and then to the left. Your arms should remain where they are. Breathe slowly, deeply, and deliberately while performing the hip movements.

Move your hips in one direction for several rounds before switching to the other direction.

If you are comfortable closing your eyes, visualize your pelvic area as a bowl of water that sways with the movements from side to side. Imagine a warm orange light shining through the water, filling the whole area with warmth, love, and calm.

Keep the hip circles up for as long as you like. Then sit back onto your heels and relax in any way that is comfortable for you.

Other beneficial activities for your sacral chakra include stimulating your creativity with a visit to a virtual art museum. Maybe you want to take up painting yourself, or brush up on your skills and stock up on your art supplies.

Free-style writing in a journal is another great stimulating activity.

Start your day with a warm cup of tea and stay hydrated throughout the day.

4

THE SOLAR PLEXUS CHAKRA—A LUSTROUS GEM

The image for the solar plexus chakra.

SUMMARY

Sanskrit name: Manipura chakra
Color: Yellow

Seed mantra: Ram

Location: Above the navel

Element: Fire

Gland: Pancreas

Psychological function: Self-confidence, self-esteem, motivation, ego, and aggression.

THE SANSKRIT NAME

The Sanskrit word manipura means "lustrous gem." The chakra is seen as the seat of energy, personal power, self-confidence, and transformation.

The Color

The yellow that is associated with the solar plexus chakra is bright like the sun, symbolizing a connection with fire, the sun, and new beginnings. The color also relates to intellect, knowledge, and cognitive energy.

The Seed Mantra

The seed mantra for the solar plexus chakra is 'ram.'

Location

The solar plexus chakra is located the breadth of about four fingers above the navel. It is believed to be a meeting place for all the nadis, or energy channels, of the body.

The manipura chakra is also associated with digestion, metabolism, and the strength of the diaphragm.

Element

The solar plexus chakra is associated with the element of fire. It maintains the momentum of that which was created by the first and second chakras, and makes sure everything functions as it should.

Manipura attracts prana, or life force, with its fiery character to balance mind and body.

The fire also refers to digestive fire—keeping the metabolism functioning well enough to digest food efficiently and provide the body's energy needs.

Gland

The solar plexus chakra relates to the pineal gland.

This is a small, pea-like structure in the middle of the brain. The function of this gland is not fully understood yet, but scientists believe it plays a big role in the body's circadian rhythms and sleeping patterns.

Psychological Function

A person with a balanced solar plexus chakra has a sense of purpose and direction. It brings motivation to carry decisions through into actions with confidence, without being arrogant.

When the chakra is out of balance, the person may have control and anger issues, be indecisive, and suffer from a low self-image.

UNDERSTANDING THE SOLAR PLEXUS CHAKRA

The manipura chakra is the seat of self-esteem, transformation, motivation, and purposeful energy.

It also rules the digestive system and metabolism.

Balance in the solar plexus chakra lights the fire of your goals and intentions, and powers up your digestion. It is about the dialogue with yourself.

THE SPIRITUAL LAW GOVERNING THE SOLAR PLEXUS CHAKRA

The law of intention and desire is associated with the solar plexus chakra.

The solar plexus is the seat of an individual's personal power. When the solar plexus chakra is open and functioning well, the person has the ability to manifest desires and dreams into concrete reality.

It is important to be aware of your intentions with your desires because, once they bear fruit in this world, they will have consequences.

WHAT CAN BLOCK THE SOLAR PLEXUS CHAKRA?

Things such as too much stress, poor life-work balance, unhealthy eating habits, bad posture, sitting for long periods of time without stretching, negative self-talk, and people-pleasing behaviors can all contribute to a blocked solar plexus chakra.

SIGNS OF AN UNBALANCED SOLAR PLEXUS CHAKRA

The signs of a blocked solar plexus chakra include the following:

Physically

Fatigue, weight gain, digestive disorders, abdominal pain, diabetes, and hypoglycemia can result from a blocked solar plexus chakra.

Psychologically

Indecision, lack of motivation, low self-esteem, too much emphasis on the ego, and no self-confidence can occur when the third chakra is blocked or out of balance.

RESTORING BALANCE AND HEALING THE SOLAR PLEXUS CHAKRA

Provided you have the intention and commitment to open and balance your chakra, there are several things you can do to help you achieve that.

Move Vigorously

While dance and movement help all the chakras, a vigorous, high-energy dance routine that recalls the warrior dances of the Mediterranean and South America will benefit the solar plexus chakra in particular. Purposeful, strong, and dramatic movements that build energy as they accelerate will ignite this chakra.

Light a Flame

Meditating with a candle or camp fire can help you reignite your spark and harness the fire locked into the solar plexus chakra.

Eat Light

Eating meals that digest easily will help to balance the solar plexus chakra. Once energy is flowing freely again, it will be easy to digest heavier foods.

Wear Yellow

Use the color yellow in your clothes and surroundings as often as you can to stimulate this chakra's energy.

Get Some Sun

Be sure to get enough sunshine while working on your third chakra. The physical heat and brightness stimulates the fires within your soul and wakes up the energy of the third chakra.

Trust Your Gut

Your solar plexus and its associated chakra can help you make decisions and choose between different possibilities to reach an outcome that is best for you.

Whenever you are faced with a difficult choice, close your eyes and place your hands over your solar plexus. Think about your dilemma or choice and notice the sensation forming in your body.

Do you feel light, almost as if you're suddenly breathing easier? Then it is the right choice for you.

If you feel heavy and nauseous and uncomfortable, it will not be the right decision to take.

Breathing Exercise

- Sit comfortably with your spine straight and your shoulders relaxed.
- Close your eyes and take a couple of deep breaths through your nose with your mouth closed.
- Next, forcefully inhale through your nose and inflate your abdomen at the same time.
- Force the breath out through your nose while flattening your abdomen toward your spine.
- The breathing should be in rapid succession, taking half a second for the inhalation and half a second for the exhalation. It should feel like you're getting an abdominal workout.
- Start with 10 repetitions and work it up to 15 or 20.
- After finishing, you should feel a warm, tingling feeling around your navel.

Yoga

Practice these asanas, or poses, to help with balancing the solar plexus chakra:

Paschimottanasana/Seated Forward Fold Pose

The aim of this pose is to relax the body as much as possible, instead of straining to reach as far forward as you can.

- Start from a seated position with your legs stretched out in front of you.
- Raise both your arms straight up and bring them back down with your hands on either side of your legs.
- Round your spine and curl your chin down to your chest while keeping your neck relaxed.
- Breathe deeply and slowly.
- Don't strain your upper back, but keep the position as relaxed as possible for a few moments.
- Lift your head, take a few deep breaths, and repeat the pose.

Dhanurasana/Bow Pose

See the discussion about the bow pose in the chapter about the sacral chakra.

Ardha Matsyendrasana/Half Spinal Twist

This excellent seated spinal stretch is also known as Half Lord of the Fishes pose. It stimulates digestion while improving posture.

- Sit on the floor or a yoga mat with your legs stretched out in front of you.
- Bend your knees while keeping your feet flat on the floor.
- Slide your left foot under your right leg all the way through to the outside of your hip.
- Lay the outside of your left leg flat on the floor.
- Lift your right foot over your left leg and put your right foot flat on the floor at the outside of your left hip. Your right knee will be pointing straight toward the ceiling.
- On an exhalation, twist your torso toward the inside of your right thigh.
- Press your right hand flat down on the floor behind your right hip and place your left upper arm on your right leg, on the outside of your right thigh and close to your knee.
- Pull your right inner thigh close to your torso. If you find that difficult to do, sit with your back about a foot away from a wall. Reach back toward the wall with your arm almost fully extended. Push the wall away when twisting to pull your thigh and torso closer together.
- Press your right foot down on the floor actively while relaxing your right groin area.
- Get a feeling of lengthening the front torso and lean the back torso back slightly; feel that your tailbone is lengthening into the floor.
- You can turn your head either right or left, whichever direction provides the stretch you need at that moment.
- Keep breathing evenly; on every exhalation, twist your torso a little bit more and lift your sternum a little bit

higher. Do not concentrate the twist and stretch in the lower back, but distribute it over the length of the spine.
- Hold the pose for 30 seconds to one minute before relaxing and repeating the stretch to the other side.

Navasana/Boat Pose

Boat pose strengthens the core muscles. Powerful abdominal muscles make many other yoga poses much easier.

The pose also stretches and strengthens the hip flexors that get tight from sitting too much. Flexible hips are important to maintain balance.

- Sit with your knees bent and your feet flat on the floor.
- Keeping your knees bent, lift your feet off the floor high enough to bring your shins into a position parallel to the floor. That is the half boat position.
- While it is naturally for your torso to fall backward, you should keep your spine straight.
- Straighten your legs into a 45-degree angle if you are flexible enough to do so without bending your upper body. There should always be a V-shape between your thighs and your body.
- Keeping the spine and torso straight is more important in this pose than fully straightening the legs. Rather do the half boat position until your flexibility and strength have improved enough.

- Holding on to the backs of your thighs with your hands can also help to keep the spine straight.
- Practicing the pose with a resistance band, or other strong elastic strap looped under the soles of your feet while holding the ends in your hands and pushing your flexed feet against the band, will also help to keep your balance until your legs are stronger.
- Straighten your arms to be roughly parallel to the floor and roll your shoulders back. Keep your palms turned upward.
- Lift your chest to keep your balance, supporting your weight on your sit bones or just slightly behind them.
- Stay in the pose for at least five breaths.
- Straighten your legs on an exhalation; inhale and sit up.

Purvottanasana/Reverse Plank Pose

Another great core strengthening position, reverse plank pose opens up the whole front of the body. It counters the tightness that can result in the shoulders and chest from sitting hunched over a computer all day.

- Sit on the floor or a yoga mat with your legs stretched out in front of you.
- Place your hands a few inches behind your hips on the floor; your fingers should be pointing toward your feet.
- Bend your knees while keeping your feet flat on the floor and your toes facing forward.
- On an exhalation, press your hands and feet down and lift your hips toward the ceiling.

- Be sure to keep your arms directly under your shoulders and your arms straight, like your legs.
- Push your chest up and lengthen your neck without forcing any muscles.
- If it is comfortable for you, allow your head to lean back.
- Stay in the position for 10 breaths.
- On an exhalation, bend your elbows and knees and lower your body.

Surya Mudra/Sun Mudra

The sun mudra is used to enhance the element of fire in the body. It is also known as agni (vardhaka) mudra ("fire (increasing) gesture") or prithvi shamak mudra ("earth reducing gesture").

The ring finger is seen as a symbol of the earth element, while the thumb represents the fire element. The use of these two fingers in the sun mudra balances the two elements in the body.

The posture should be done before sunrise to utilize the sun's energy, or before eating. If it is done after a meal, 45 minutes to an hour should elapse in between.

- Sit comfortably on a yoga mat, such as in a lotus or half lotus position.
- Place your hands on your knees or thighs with your palms facing upward.
- Close your eyes and breathe deeply and evenly.
- Bend your ring finger and touch the tip of it to the tip of your thumb.

- Slide your ring finger down the length of your thumb until you touch the root of your thumb.
- The other three fingers should remain extended.
- Apply some pressure on your ring finger with your thumb—don't overdo it, keep it comfortable, but the pressure has to be enough to show some white on your fingertips.
- Keep the mudra for about five minutes, longer if you can.

Rudra Mudra/Mudra Associated With a Rigvedic Deity Called Rudra

The Sanskrit word 'rudra' also means 'terror' or 'howler,' and the mudra is associated with the powerful Hindu god Shiva, pointing to the relationship with self-confidence in the solar plexus chakra.

- In a seated position, place your hands with the palms facing upward on your thighs.
- Touch the tips of your ring fingers, index fingers, and thumbs on both hands together.
- Straighten the middle fingers and pinkies as much as is comfortable.

Gemstones and Crystals

Several of the stones and crystals that can be used with the sacral chakra will also be beneficial for the solar plexus chakra. Just look for the more yellow hues, as these stones occur in shades ranging from pale yellow to brown.

Citrine

The bright yellow of this sparkling stone that looks like frozen sunlight resonates very well with the solar plexus chakra. It aids self-belief and helps to cultivate a motivated mindset to push through with your goals.

It helps you to stand strong against pleasing people at the cost of your own truth and self-esteem.

Pyrite (Fool's Gold)

The name of this mineral comes from the Greek word 'pyr,' which means 'fire.' That makes it an ideal choice for the solar plexus chakra.

Pyrite can help you block negative energy, stopping outside forces from affecting your positive mood and eroding your confidence. That keeps your thoughts centered on success and helps you retain clarity in reasoning.

Peridot

Although peridot is not yellow, its green hue is so close to yellow that it is sometimes difficult to decide which color it really is. The color makes it an effective bridge between the solar plexus and heart chakras.

Peridot energizes and cleans, bringing forgiveness and healing hurts. It helps you release negative thought patterns that may have become entrenched, resulting in negative behaviors that slow down progress.

The stone helps you to let go of past experiences after learning from them, to move forward with renewed confidence.

Tiger's Eye

The brown version of tiger's eye might be better known, but there is a beautiful yellow tiger's eye as well.

It cleans and heals the solar plexus chakra from fears that hold you back. It can help to balance mood swings and replenish low energy stores.

Tiger's eye combines the energies of the earth and the sun. It is a powerful combination that guides you to take action based on your gut feelings.

Amber

Amber's strong connection with the earth as fossilized tree resin counters overactivity in the solar plexus chakra that can bring about mood swings, frustration, and manic emotional episodes.

It boosts patience and absorbs anger, bringing balance and harmony to the third chakra.

Amber can also open your mind to ancient wisdom.

Yellow Jasper

Yellow Jasper is a grounding stone that affords protection against negative emotions from others such as jealousy.

It boosts confidence to speak up and finish projects.

This is a stone that vibrates at a low frequency, so its effect will not be felt immediately. It needs to be used steadily over a long time to fully enjoy its benefits.

Heliodor

This is a type of beryl that is also known as golden or yellow beryl. Its name means "gift from the sun" in Greek and it bestows clarity of vision and rich variety in thought. That will help you make difficult decisions and boost self-confidence.

Heliodor also helps to restore depleted mental energy when you feel burned out.

Golden Yellow Topaz

The rare yellow variety of topaz is also called imperial topaz. It is an amplifying stone that draws energy through the third chakra to wherever it is needed and boosts drive and confidence.

It also promotes connections with the right people at the right time and boosts your social life with deep friendships.

Yellow Smithsonite

This stone is the friend of your inner child. It brings compassion and stability to remove the memories of any childhood traumas that block confidence and sabotage relationships.

It can soothe worries and negative feelings, making it possible to drop defensive barriers safely. This will open the way for your beautiful higher self to shine through.

Golden Healer Quartz

The iron oxide trapped within this quartz gives it a rich, yellow color. It is a powerful aid to open all the energy channels so healing can take place on all levels.

It boosts any efforts to acquire new habits and help ensure, by raising your personal vibrations, that the changes are permanent.

It can help you work through any trust issues that prevent you from stepping into your personal power and restore your self-esteem and confidence.

Orpiment

> **A word of caution: This stone contains arsenic. Wash your hands immediately after using it and do not carry it in your pockets or clothing. Also, beware of it falling and splintering because it is a very brittle stone.**

All of that said, orpiment is still a powerful aid to restore balance to the solar plexus chakra and boost self-confidence. It can activate your will to become aligned with your emotions and desires, thereby creating a strong focus on positive results.

In activating and balancing the solar plexus chakra, all emotional baggage that prevents you from realizing your full potential can be booted out, and focusing on your aspirations becomes far less stressful.

Yellow Aventurine

These tiny, bright yellow quartz stones can enhance decisiveness and confidence, boost personal courage, and help you find balance between your personal power and the control you exert.

It brings a certain amount of playfulness to leadership and decreases any oversensitivity.

The stone will strengthen your focus on issues that are worth your time and effort and bring you peace and calm because you are making the right decisions.

Yellow Jade

This is an extremely rare variety of jade and can be found in shades from dark yellow to pale lemon yellow.

Yellow jade stimulates digestion and can give your metabolism a boost.

On the emotional side, the stone will stimulate courage, self-confidence, and wisdom. It will enhance focus while helping you to keep a balance between work and free time.

Yellow Fluorite

Fluorite is a highly sought-after crystal with a very ordered internal matrix. Its near-perfection in nature affords it an ability to calm and order the human mind when used metaphysically.

Yellow, or golden, fluorite enhances imagination, intellectual abilities, and resourcefulness. It strengthens any intentions set and helps you to realize them for the higher good.

It is an excellent stone to align us with higher truths and make them more understandable to our human consciousness. It helps us to see and interpret cues from the universe and put them into action.

Golden Mookaite

This is a unique gemstone, a type of jasper found only on the banks of the Mooka Creek, in the Kennedy mountain range of western Australia. It is believed to have a strong connection to the earth's electromagnetic field.

It imparts grounding and boosts connection between all living beings. That will help you to grab every opportunity and make the most of it because you are fully present and aware.

The stone opens and balances the solar plexus chakra so that personal power can be accessed and controlled.

Brucite

This stone helps to strengthen inner convictions against outer forces of social society and family pressure. That opens the way for our intuition and innate, ancient wisdom to emerge and guide us to fulfill our potential.

Essential Oils and Herbs

Woody and sweet scents work well to balance and heal the solar plexus chakra. Oils such as sandalwood, cedarwood, lemongrass, ylang ylang, myrrh, lavender, helichrysum, lily of the valley, juniper, grapefruit, tea tree, anise, celery, cinnamon, turmeric, black pepper, and cumin are good choices.

Foods

Any foods in this chakra's color of yellow will be beneficial. Pineapples, lemons, yellow bell peppers, bananas, and corn.

Whole grains and complex carbohydrates that will provide sustained energy such as spelt, rye, oats, brown rice, sprouted grains, and beans are good choices to balance the solar plexus chakra.

The fire element that resonates with the solar plexus chakra also calls for sour, salt, or pungent foods—anything with a strong taste. Think garlic, onions, peppers, chilies, ginger, turmeric, cinnamon, oregano, soy sauce, fermented foods, vinegar, and alcohol.

Affirmations

Here are a few suggestions for affirmations to get you started.

- I have the conviction to make my own decisions.
- I trust my own decisions.
- I give myself full permission to be authentic and true to myself.

- I am motivated to pursue my goals.
- I believe in the power of my goals.
- I release all need to be in control in every situation.
- I am confident that I have everything I need within me.
- I release my past.
- I am worthy of the life I design for myself and I give myself permission to enjoy that life.
- I have much to offer the world.

A Guided Meditation

Use the following guided meditation to balance and heal your solar plexus chakra.

Hold the solar plexus chakra gemstones or crystals while you meditate, or arrange them around you. Build yourself a mandala by placing gemstones, herbs, and spices around or near you to enhance the effect of your meditation.

Record the script for this meditation on your cell phone to make meditating easy. Just remember to read slowly and give yourself enough time to move from step to step.

> *Find a comfortable position in a favorite chair, on a yoga mat, or a bed.*
> *Fold your hands loosely in your lap and keep your feet relaxed on the floor if you are sitting.*
> *If you are lying down, keep your legs straight and don't cross your ankles. Keep your arms next to your body on the bed or fold your hands over your midsection.*

Place a pillow under your knees if you need it for comfort. With your eyes closed, become aware of the textures that touch your body...do they feel warm, soft, cool, smooth? Concentrate the sensations in a bright yellow ball that is forming in the middle of your body. See them all rolling into the ball and feel their touch fading.
See yourself lifting from where you are lying or sitting by the yellow ball of energy that is carrying you on wings like an eagle.
You are soaring in power, free from bondage.
Breathe in the freshness of freedom...and exhale all feelings of powerlessness and frustration.
And breathe in freedom and power...and exhale frustration. Savor the feeling for as long as you like.
[Pause]
When you feel ready, stir your arms and legs and slowly become aware of the sounds of the outside world again.
Open your eyes.

Music

Music specifically composed for balancing the solar plexus chakra can be accessed freely at several places online. These include:

- https://www.youtube.com/watch?v=O7o0pEoKMBg
- https://www.youtube.com/watch?v=4ZzXZS5q6bk

With regards to contemporary music, any piece in the key of E will resonate with the solar plexus chakra.

"Africa," by Toto, "Norwegian Wood," by The Beatles, "Just Dance," by Lady Gaga, "My Heart Will Go On," by Céline Dion, "Isn't She Lovely," by Stevie Wonder, "If You Leave Me Now," by Peter Cetera, "Barracuda," by Heart, "Born to Run," by Bruce Springsteen, "Little Sister," by Elvis Presley, and "Adeste Fideles," by Bing Crosby are all in this key.

Other Activities

Make a short daily walk or a regular yoga session part of your schedule to see great results with this chakra.

- Kickstart your motivation by setting goals and drawing up a weekly to-do list for yourself. Keep track of your achievements and ask a friend or family member to hold you accountable.
- Reward yourself for every goal accomplished, no matter how small it might be.
- If your eating habits are not healthy, change to nourishing meals that you can prepare from scratch at home, or order from a farm-to-table restaurant.
- Expand your tastes in food and be adventurous. Find new tastes to nurture your body.
- Enjoy beverages at room temperature or only slightly warmed instead of chilled. Avoid adding ice. That will help strengthen your digestive fire.
- If you need something to drink during meals, take small sips of water. Stay away from soda, fruit juice, and alcohol that will increase acid levels in the body.

- Don't overeat and give your stomach enough time to rest between meals.

5

THE HEART CHAKRA—THE UNBEATEN

The image for the heart chakra.

SUMMARY

Sanskrit name: Anahata chakra
Color: Green

Seed mantra: Yam

Location: The heart region in the center of the chest

Element: Air

Gland: Thymus

Psychological function: Love, attachment, compassion, trust, and passion

THE SANSKRIT NAME

The Sanskrit word 'anahata' means something that is unhurt and unbeaten. That brings to mind the purity of heart that an open heart chakra promotes.

The Color

The color green is associated with the heart chakra. It signifies renewal in both self-growth and relationships.

It is also a restful shade for the human eye, bringing serenity and balance.

The Seed Mantra

The seed mantra for the heart chakra is 'yam.' It means to liberate and let go, and to give freely.

Location

It is located at the center of the chest, in the area where the physical heart is. That points to its pivotal role as a link between the lower and higher chakras.

It is also central to our experiences in the physical plane, bringing the perspective of the divine to bear.

Element

The heart chakra is associated with the element of air. Air symbolizes freedom from restrictions.

A balanced and healthy anahata chakra allows us to love and give without any conditions and restrictions, remaining optimistic even in the face of hardships.

Gland

The heart chakra relates to the thymus gland. It is a lymphoid gland, located in the chest, that is important in the immune system.

Psychological Function

A balanced heart chakra creates feelings of openness to give and receive unconditional love. It restores the connection with our fellow human beings, but also with divine energy and spiritual wisdom.

It opens us up to compassion and kindness toward all beings as well as ourselves.

The heart chakra functions as a bridge between the lower and higher chakras, uniting our physical existence with the spiritual realities we often lose sight of.

UNDERSTANDING THE HEART CHAKRA

The heart chakra is sometimes called "the seat of the soul" because of its central position in emotions such as love, compassion, kindness, generosity, optimism, and motivation.

To establish true, loving connections between people, and between us and the energy of the divine source of life, the heart chakra has to be open and fully functional.

THE SPIRITUAL LAW GOVERNING THE HEART CHAKRA

The heart chakra is governed by the law of giving and receiving. It strives for unity and connection among all beings in life.

Giving and receiving cannot be separated from each other. By doing the one, you provide the opportunity for the other to take place. It is a two-way street and doing one opens the road for the other one.

WHAT CAN BLOCK THE HEART CHAKRA?

Stress, worry, and depression all block love, which blocks the energy of the heart chakra. Hate, mistrust, and spite are also negative emotions that will adversely affect the health and balance of the heart chakra.

SIGNS OF AN UNBALANCED HEART CHAKRA

There are telltale signs of a blocked heart chakra.

Physically

Low energy, fatigue, heart palpitations, angina, pain in the heart region, poor blood circulation, and even asthma can result from a blocked heart chakra.

Psychologically

A gloomy, pessimistic outlook on life, feelings of hopelessness, rejection, and hopelessness indicate a dysfunctional heart chakra.

In a stable relationship, loss of trust, abnormal dependency, and difficulty giving and receiving affection can occur.

RESTORING BALANCE AND HEALING THE HEART CHAKRA

Provided you have the intention and commitment to open and balance your chakra, there are several things you can do to help you achieve that.

Move Your Arms

When dancing or exercising for this chakra, concentrate on movements where the arms can be lifted and waved, freeing the joyful, compassionate energy of the heart chakra.

Meet Yourself

Write yourself a love letter and go on a date with yourself.

Be honest about the things you love about yourself; no one else ever has to see the letter.

That beautiful person is the one you will become, if you allow yourself.

Volunteer

Become involved in charity or community projects that make a difference in the lives of others, without any monetary compensation.

Do a Metta Meditation

The word 'metta' comes from an Indian language that is closely related to Sanskrit. It means 'kindness.'

Visualize yourself sitting across from you and vocalize good wishes for yourself. These could include phrases such as, "may I be safe," "may I be joyful," and "may I know love."

Next, visualize someone you love in the same seat and wish them the same as you did for yourself.

Lastly, imagine a person with whom you have conflict sitting across from you. Wish them the same good things you did for yourself and your loved one.

Breathing Exercise

The breathing exercise, or pranayama, called bhramari/humming bee breathing is an effective way to clear stress, anger, and anxiety from the heart and allow the anahata chakra to function again as it should.

The Indian word 'bhramari' means 'bee' and refers to a species of black humming bee occurring in that country. The breathing technique imitates the buzzing sound of a bee.

Settle yourself comfortably in a seated position with your eyes closed. Place your index fingers on the cartilage between your ears and cheeks.

Breathe in deeply and, as you breathe out, gently close your ears with your fingers while making a bzzz-sound like a bee. A slightly higher pitch works better than a low pitch.

Repeat the breathing pattern for about five times.

Yoga

Practice these asanas, or poses, to help with balancing the heart chakra:

Salamba Bhujangasana/Sphinx Pose

See the discussion of the sphinx pose in the chapter on the sacral chakra.

Bhujangasana/Cobra Pose

The cobra pose was discussed briefly as part of the sun salutations, in the chapter on the root chakra.

Let's look at it in more detail now.

The cobra pose is very similar to the sphinx pose and is also excellent for opening up the chest and stretching the shoulders.

- Begin by lying down on your stomach on a yoga mat.
- Put your palms flat on the floor next to your chest and keep your elbows close to your body. Your fingertips should be in line with the tops of your shoulders.
- Lift your upper body off the mat by pushing on your hands, feeling the stretch down all the muscles along your spine.
- Making sure your elbows stay close to your sides, press your shoulder blades closer to each other.
- Expand your chest by pulling yourself further up and forward.
- Draw your shoulders away from your ears and imagine your neck lengthening.
- Be sure to lift the base of your skull also away from your shoulders.
- Stay in the position for as long as is comfortable to you before lowering your chest and resting your body.

Anjaneyasana/Low Lunge

This position is also known as the crescent moon pose. It energizes the heart and heart chakra because it opens up the chest.

- Begin the low lunge pose from the V-shape of the downward facing dog pose.
- Bring your right foot forward to a position between your hands and bend your right knee to align it above your right heel.
- Carefully lower your left knee to the ground too.
- Slide your left knee back until you feel your hip flexor stretch while keeping your right leg still.
- Draw your tailbone down to the floor and lift your pelvic bone toward your navel.
- Lift your arms up into a frame for your head and stretch them to lift your chest too.
- Keep pressing your shoulder blades toward each other while keeping your shoulders relaxed.
- Gaze upward for five breaths before switching sides.

Ashta Chandrasana/Crescent High Lunge

This position is done by hooking the thumbs of the uplifted hands together. The name comes from the resemblance between the silhouette of the body during the pose, and the shape of the moon when waxing or waning.

- Start the crescent high lunge in the same way as the low

lunge. Assume the V-shape of the downward facing dog pose and bring your right foot forward to a position between your hands.

- Keep your weight on the ball of your left foot and angle your right knee at 90 degrees over your ankle.
- Raise your upper body slowly and carefully while keeping your shoulders aligned with your hips.
- Reach both your arms straight up and hook your thumbs around each other.
- Move your gaze up to your thumbs and slowly start going into a backbend.
- Use your legs as a firm foundation for the bend, push your pelvic floor up, and draw your navel in.
- Hold the position for five breaths before coming back into a downward facing dog pose.
- Repeat the pose to the other side.

Natarajasana/Dancer's Pose/Lord of the Dance Pose

This position comes from classical Indian temple dances and can be quite challenging for a beginner. It is essential to warm up properly with stretches and other asanas first before attempting the dancer's pose.

It opens the chest and front of the body while enhancing focus and stability.

- Start this pose by assuming the mountain pose on your yoga mat.

- Shift your weight to your right foot on an inhalation.
- Keep your right leg strong by pulling up your knee cap and pushing your thigh bone up into the hip joint.
- Lift your left foot slowly and carefully off the mat, making sure you keep your balance.
- Bring your foot closer to your left glute and take hold of the inside of your foot with your left hand.
- Stretch your right arm straight out before you, parallel to the floor.
- Press with your left foot into your left hand and lean your upper body forward as far as is comfortable for you.
- Keep the position for 20 to 30 seconds.
- Release your hold on your left foot, lower it to the floor, and repeat the pose for the other side.

Garudasana/Eagle Arms Pose

The eagle arms pose is part of the eagle pose that involves the legs too.

The position stretches the arms and chest and enhances balance when the full position is assumed. Eagle arms pose is an excellent antidote after spending hours sitting in front of a computer. It can even be done without getting up from your desk.

- Stretch both your arms straight out in front of you, parallel with the floor or desk.
- Bend your arms and cross your left arm over the right, hooking your elbows.

- Draw your forearms closer to each other and cross your wrists to wrap your right palm around your left palm.
- Keep your spine straight and the crown of your head reaching toward the ceiling.
- For added shoulder stretch, you can lift your elbows to the level of your shoulders. Remember to keep your shoulders away from your ears.

Salabhasana/Locust Pose

This position strengthens the arms and the entire back body, and opens up the chest.

The backbend is shallow and that makes the pose accessible to most people.

- Lie on your stomach on your yoga mat with your arms at your sides, your palms facing downward, and your forehead on the mat.
- Keep your hips and lower belly on the mat while lifting your legs, head, and chest a few inches from the mat. If you have back problems, try one leg first until your muscles are flexible enough for you to progress to lifting both legs at the same time.
- Keep your knees straight.
- Lift your arms to be parallel to the mat.
- Imagine your upper body lengthening from your hips up to your crown, and your lower body lengthening from your hips to the soles of your feet.

- Keep the position for five breaths before lowering your whole body again.
- The pose can also be done by lifting the legs only, or the upper body only.

Ustrasana/Camel Pose

This pose is done kneeling, and the backbend opens the chest and lifts the rib cage. It also strengthens and tones the quadriceps and abdomen.

It is an intermediate position that is more accessible to more people than some of the other backbend poses. It can also be done by those with weaker arm strength because the weight is not supported on the arms.

- Start in a kneeling position with your upper body straight and your hips positioned over your knees.
- Slide your hands up along the sides of your body until you reach your rib cage.
- Place your thumbs on the back of your ribs and curl your other fingers around the sides and front. Your elbows should be pointing outward.
- Push your chest up toward the ceiling, opening it up.
- Use your hands as supports, helping you to lift your rib cage.
- Reach back with one hand at a time to grasp your heels. If you can't reach your heels, keep your hands on your lower back.
- Tuck your toes in for a bit of added height if you need it;

otherwise, you can keep your toes flat on the mat. You can also position yoga blocks on either side of your feet to help.
- Keep your hips over your knees—shift them slightly forward if needed.
- It is important to keep your thighs straight to reap the full benefits of the camel pose. If you are exercising alone with no one to check your alignment, position yourself with the front of your thighs against a wall. Your thighs should stay in contact with the wall all the time while you are bending backward, to prevent your body from just slanting back.
- Roll your head back to open your throat if your neck is comfortable with the movement and position. If not, keep your chin tucked in.
- Hold the position for five breaths.
- Release the pose by dropping your chin back to your chest, supporting your lower back with your hands, and slowly return to the same upright kneeling position from which you started.

Padma Mudra/Lotus Mudra

The lotus flower is seen as a symbol of overcoming adverse circumstances to bloom beautifully in love, enlightenment, and self-knowledge.

Use the lotus hand gesture to symbolize this opening-up process.

- Put your palms together with your hands at your heart.
- Separate the tips of your index, middle, and ring fingers

while your thumbs, pinkies, and the heels of your palms remain touching.
- Allow your fingers to blossom open like a lotus.
- Extend the stretch through all your fingers.

Gemstones and Crystals

Several stones and crystals resonate with the heart chakra.

Rose Quartz

The king of love is undoubtedly rose. The vibrant pink stone can purify and deepen relationships and open up the heart to encourage healing.

It strengthens empathy and replaces any negative vibrations with the higher vibrations of love, acceptance, and compassion.

The stone can help the heart chakra to release long-held emotional wounds and traumas to lift your spirit, letting you soar on the wings of close and fulfilling relationships—both with others and yourself.

Emerald

The pure and brilliant green color of an emerald makes it a favorite gemstone for opening and healing the heart chakra.

The stone boosts partnerships and balances relationships. It makes it easier to recover from negative energies and experiences, replacing them with a renewed capacity for joy.

Emerald will also boost wisdom and compassion, bringing people in relationships closer together than they ever were.

Rhodochrosite

This is a useful stone to remove emotional blockages and self-doubt. Its planetary ruler is Venus, the planet of love.

It also helps to reconnect with the self, when self-love has suffered due to emotional traumas.

Green Aventurine

Green aventurine emits a soft energy that soothes friction while bringing clarity about hurtful and damaging behaviors. It opens relationships up to new opportunities for connection.

It can shield the aura from energy vampires and any other negative emotional energies.

The stone promotes a feeling of well-being and enhances your focus on things that really matter to you.

Malachite

Malachite is also known as a stone of transformation. Its powerful vibrations bring about a shift in the heart chakra, helping you to release negative energy and blocks and replace them with stable, loving, and balanced energy.

It is a great aid for anyone who feels very deeply, such as empaths, to move past being overwhelmed by other people's emotions.

Rhodonite

This stone encourages forgiveness and compromise. It balances emotions and brings harmony where it might be lacking.

Rhodonite makes it possible to transform pain into love and move forward again. It helps to replace any self-doubt with confidence.

Green Jade

The green variety of jade is perhaps the best known of the jade family of gemstones. It can protect against negativity while boosting patience and tolerance in relationships.

Green jade sets the imagination free, allowing relationships to grow in unexpected ways.

Prehnite

This stone enhances personal peace and a calm disposition, helping to ease worries and dispel emotional distress.

Amazonite

Amazonite acts as a bridge between the love of the heart chakra and the self-expression of the throat chakra.

It can help to get insight into a relationship with a controlling partner and empower you to express your truths and boundaries in love.

The stone brings clarity about emotional issues without falling into the trap of self-doubt.

Pink Tourmaline

This stone is known as a calming aid. It can soften emotional pain and help to release anxiety.

It is also believed to energize the heart chakra with the motivation to make its loving intentions concrete in relationships.

Chrysoprase

This stone is also known as the healer of broken hearts. It has the unique ability to help equalize emotional balances, making it possible to accept change and come out stronger and more loving than ever before.

It boosts self-esteem while balancing it with tolerance for others.

Essential Oils and Herbs

Parsley, thyme, cilantro, marjoram, cacao, cardamom, rose, neroli, pine, hawthorn, jasmine, bergamot, lavender, and mint are powerful aids to open and balance the heart chakra.

Foods

Green and raw are the words for the heart chakra. Salads, green juices, and green smoothies will all do nicely. Celery, cucumber, zucchini, spinach, broccoli, Brussels sprouts, kale, chard, lime, avocado, peas, spirulina, and green apples can be considered.

Astringent and bitter foods also work well with the element of air. Red wine, green tea, and pomegranate seeds are all astringent. Coffee and dark chocolate make up the bitter complement.

Affirmations

Here are a few suggestions for affirmations to get you started.

- I welcome love into my life.
- I am successful in love.
- I am not afraid to open myself up in relationships.
- I attract love and light.
- I am worthy of unconditional love and I love myself freely.
- I let go of past hurts and anything else that doesn't serve me any longer.
- I feel safe to love.
- My heart is overflowing with joy and gratitude.
- Love guides all my actions.
- My mistakes are stepping stones and I learn from them.

A Guided Meditation

Use the following guided meditation to balance and heal your heart chakra and to live from its place of unconditional love.

Hold the heart chakra gemstones or crystals while you meditate, or arrange them around you. Build yourself a mandala by placing gemstones, herbs, and spices around or near you to enhance the effect of your meditation.

Record the script for this meditation on your cell phone to make meditating easy. Just remember to read slowly and give yourself enough time to move from step to step.

If you can, meditate in nature where you are surrounded by green.

Sit or lie down comfortably where you will not be disturbed for about half an hour.

Keep your feet next to each other on the floor if you are sitting. Don't cross your ankles if you are lying down.

Keep your arms and hands relaxed by your sides or in your lap.

Close your eyes.

Breathe naturally and calmly for a few deep breaths...in through the nose...out through the mouth.

And in through the nose...out through the mouth.

Visualize a clear and brilliant green point of light penetrating and filling the center of your heart.

While breathing deeply and calmly, visualize the point of brilliant green light expanding to fill your whole heart with soft light. Feel its nurturing, caring energy envelop your heart.

Breathe naturally and calmly for a few deep breaths...in through the nose...out through the mouth.

And in through the nose...out through the mouth.

Imagine the soft, green light pushing out any negativity and hurt with every exhalation and replacing it with loving energy.

See your whole chest immersed in its caring green glow, radiating from you to the universe.

Breathe in the soft caring light...and exhale all darkness.

Savor the light for as long as you like.

[Pause]

When you feel ready, stir your arms and legs and slowly become aware of the sounds of the outside world again. Open your eyes.

Music

Music specifically composed for balancing the heart chakra can be accessed freely at several places online. These include:

https://www.youtube.com/watch?v=s1pG7k_1nSw

https://www.youtube.com/watch?v=8nSPy3ifSoE

Other music in the key of D that resonates with the heart chakra include "Wish You Were Here," by Pink Floyd, "Annie's Song," by John Denver, "While My Guitar Gently Weeps," by George Harrison, "I Can See Clearly Now," by Johnny Nash, "Love Changes Everything," by the Royal Philharmonic Orchestra, "Bless the Wings (That Bring You Back)," by The Moody Blues, "If I Should Love Again," by Barry Manilow, "Kung Fu Fighting," by Carl Douglas, "Just the Way You Are," by Billy Joel, and "Return To Me (Ritorna-Me)," by Dean Martin.

Other Activities

Random acts of kindness toward friends and strangers are completely up the alley of the heart chakra. Send a neighbor flowers or buy coffee for the stranger in the car behind you at the drive-thru.

Start a gratitude journal and find five things you are grateful for, as well as one person you appreciate in your life, every day.

Make stillness your friend and spend more time just breathing deeply and easily.

THE THROAT CHAKRA—THE PURIFIER

The image for the throat chakra.

SUMMARY

Sanskrit name: Vishuddha chakra
Color: Blue

Seed mantra: Ham
Location: Base of the throat
Element: Ether/space
Gland: Thyroid
Psychological function: Inspiration, expression, faith, and the ability to communicate

THE SANSKRIT NAME

The word 'visshuddha' means "especially pure." It signifies the truthful communication that comes naturally when the throat chakra is functioning as it should.

The Color

Blue is associated with the throat chakra. It symbolizes purity, healing, calm, and expansion.

The Seed Mantra

The seed mantra for the throat chakra is 'ham.'

Location

It is located at the base of the throat, at the center of the larynx. That is one of the gateways into and out of the body.

Element

The throat chakra is associated with the element of ether or space. Space is limitless and free, and so should we live, talk, and think too.

Gland

The throat chakra relates to the thyroid. This butterfly-shaped gland in the front part of the neck forms an essential part of all metabolic processes in the body, and when it is diseased, many vital functions that support life are in danger.

Psychological function

A healthy and active throat chakra enables a person to listen and communicate on a different level. The heart and mind is purified from harmful intentions and interpretations, allowing authentic expression and honest communication.

This also relates to body language and not only verbal communication.

UNDERSTANDING THE THROAT CHAKRA

When the throat chakra is not functioning well, toxic elements interfere with the body and mind.

This chakra rules communication between ourselves and the divine, ourselves and others, and ourselves with our true selves. It is about talking, but also about knowing when to keep quiet and just understand.

It is all about purity of intention and body, and living true to our divine purpose without apologies.

THE SPIRITUAL LAW GOVERNING THE THROAT CHAKRA

The spiritual law of detachment is associated with the throat chakra. That means a person with an open and active throat chakra is free from worry and fear about other people's judgments about what they say. It does not mean saying anything you like and hurting people—on the contrary. Truths and needs are expressed in a way that supports others while remaining truthful.

This law is a constant reminder that we can trust the universe to take care of people's responses to our words and actions, if we choose our words with pure intentions and a loving, truthful heart.

WHAT CAN BLOCK THE THROAT CHAKRA?

Polluted air and unhealthy eating habits will throw this chakra off balance in the physical sense. Being forced to hide one's true self or being dishonest and insincere will do the same on the psychological level.

SIGNS OF AN UNBALANCED THROAT CHAKRA

The signs of a blocked throat chakra include the following:

Physically

Headaches, neck and shoulder aches, anemia, thyroid issues, throat infections, dental problems, and mouth ulcers can indicate an unbalanced throat chakra.

Psychologically

Anxiety, selfishness, gaslighting, people pleasing, lying, excessive/no talking, difficulty expressing feelings, feeling misunderstood most of the time, aggression, negative talking, and an inability to stay quiet and listen to others frequently occur when the throat chakra is unhealthy.

RESTORING BALANCE AND HEALING THE THROAT CHAKRA

Provided you have the intention and commitment to open and balance your chakra, there are several things you can do to help you achieve that.

Chant

Even if you only hum, use your voice to unlock and balance the power of the throat chakra.

If you combine the chant with swaying movements, the sound effect will be enhanced even more.

Sing

Singing is an active process that involves physical and emotional aspects of communication.

Listen to Music

Immerse yourself frequently in any music you find soothing, uplifting, inspiring, or just beautiful.

Meditate

While meditation is beneficial for all the chakras, the throat chakra especially benefits from frequent silent meditation.

Enjoy Soothing Drinks

A glass of lemon water or a cup of soothing herbal tea can do wonders for an unhappy throat chakra.

Breathing Exercise

Two breathing exercises can engage the throat and energize the vishuddi chakra again.

The ujjāyī pranayama is done by breathing with a slightly constricted throat, so that the breathing sounds like that of someone in deep sleep, almost snoring.

Concentrate on the sound only so that the mind quiets down and the emotions get the opportunity to balance themselves.

Keep breathing like this for five to 10 minutes.

The effect of the ujjāyī pranayama can be strengthened by doing a **jālandhara bandha** (throat lock) at the same time. While exhaling, place your hands on your knees and tilt your body forward slightly. Press your chin down on your sternum, blocking the flow of air and blood to the throat.

Hold the position until you need to inhale again, raise your head, and breathe in.

Yoga

Practice these asanas, or poses, to help with balancing the throat chakra:

Sarvangasana/Shoulder Stand ('Candle')

A note of caution: Anyone suffering from a detached retina or glaucoma should not attempt this pose—the pressure in the throat and head region can aggravate those conditions.

The shoulder stand is one of the poses known as inversions. Inversion poses are considered essential in yoga.

The shoulder stand is more beginner-friendly than the headstand while still providing the benefits of stimulating the parasympathetic nervous system, promoting good blood flow, and easing anxiety and fatigue.

The asana also stimulates the thyroid, thereby also stimulating the throat chakra.

It encourages abdominal breathing because the position limits the use of the top part of the lungs.

The shoulder stand boosts digestion because the compressing effects of gravity on the colon are released.

Core muscles are strengthened and arm and upper body strength is boosted.

- Start by lying down on a yoga mat with your arms and hands by your sides. Keep your feet together.
- Breathe in and lift both legs up to a 90 degree angle.
- Follow the leg-lift with your hips, lifting them while supporting them with your hands.
- Make sure your head and neck stay on the mat.
- Walk your hands up on your rib cage, toward your shoulder blades.
- Tuck your chin in toward your chest and lift your hips as high as you can.
- Hold your legs so that your feet will be above your head.
- Breathe slowly while focusing on your throat and the surrounding area.
- Hold the pose for five to 10 breaths, then lower your feet and replace your hands on the mat.
- Roll your body slowly out of the pose.

Halasana/Plough Pose

The same word of caution regarding eye conditions for the shoulder stand is valid for the plough pose.

The plough pose is another inversion, and it is commonly performed when coming out of a shoulder stand.

- Follow the steps for the shoulder stand, but instead of straightening your legs upward, guide them gently and in a controlled movement toward your head.
- Place your feet on the floor behind your head.

- Hold your knees straight with your feet together and flexed.
- Once your toes are comfortably settled on the floor behind you, interlock your hands on the floor behind your back to help you keep your balance.
- Breathe evenly for five to 10 times before slowly coming out of the pose by using your hands as levers on the floor, while bending your knees, and rolling your body out of the pose.

Chakravakasana/Cat-Cow Stretch With Lion's Breath

Alternating the cat and cow poses mobilizes the whole spine, while adding the so-called lion's breath stimulates the throat chakra.

The spine is moved from a rounded position to being flexed, and back, improving blood circulation around the spinal discs.

The movements are linked with inhalation on the one and exhalation on the other one.

- Start on all fours on a yoga mat.
- Position your wrists to be aligned under your shoulders and your knees under your hips.
- Visualize your spine as a rod that connects your hips and your shoulders.
- Imagine the rod extending forward through your crown and backward through your tailbone, creating a neutral position for your spine.
- Curl your toes in.
- Inhale and tilt your pelvis upward, arching your back for the cow pose.

- Your neck should be the last part of your body to move.
- Drop your belly but keep your navel tucked toward your spine with your abdominal muscles.
- Allow your gaze to travel upward slowly without extending your neck.
- Now exhale and uncurl your toes so that the tops of your feet are on the mat.
- Tilt your pelvis and tuck your tailbone down and in.
- Allow your spine to curve naturally.
- Drop your head and let your gaze travel toward your navel.
- After a few rounds of alternating between cow and cat, introduce the breathing technique known as lion's breath on your exhalations.
- It is done by forcefully releasing the breath, making a roaring sound that tones the throat.
- Stick your tongue out while roaring.

Matsyasana/Fish Pose

The fish pose is an excellent stretch for the throat, chest, upper back, abdomen, and the intercostal muscles between the ribs.

It is an easy beginner position that stretches the same muscles as the shoulder stand.

- Start by lying on your back on a yoga mat.
- Push yourself up on your elbows while keeping your forearms flat on the mat.
- Roll your shoulders back and pull your shoulder blades

toward each other to puff your chest up. Your body will automatically go into a backbend.
- If it will make you feel more stable, you can tuck your hands under your hips.
- Tilt your head back until your crown touches the floor lightly, if possible—don't rest on your crown. If your head can't reach the floor, don't force it. Leaving your head dangling can provide an equally good stretch for your spine.
- Keep your legs straight and your toes pointed.
- Keep the position for as long as you are comfortable.
- When you are ready to come out of it, pull your chin back to your chest, slide your elbows forward, and lower your whole body to the mat.

Granthita Mudra/Knot Mudra

The Sanskrit word 'granthi' means a knot that is difficult to untie. In Vedic and yogic literature, granthis are described as blocks to the life-giving energy, or pranayama. The blocks prevent the energy from rising through the central nadi to allow the person to fulfill his/her true potential.

When the throat chakra is blocked, true self-expression is blocked. That will hold a person back from becoming who they were destined to be.

The knot mudra is used to untie the block and support spiritual development.

- Hold your hands together in front of you and interlace the pinkies, ring, and middle fingers.
- Form two rings with your index fingers and thumbs, interlocking them with each other and touching the tips.
- Hold the mudra in front of the base of your throat.

Gemstones and Crystals

Several stones and crystals resonate with the throat chakra.

Amazonite

This beautiful blue-green gemstone is believed to calm nervous tension and boost emotional balance. It is also used to protect against negative energy and strengthen courage to speak out.

Lapis Lazuli

The stone of kings is used to release anger and promote honesty in both the spoken and written word.

The brilliant blue stone has been the hallmark of royalty since ancient times. It is regarded as a symbol of wisdom, leading you into wisdom and truth. When there is anger, blocking the way of truth, lapis lazuli is said to ease the irritations leading to the anger, and thereby clearing the mind.

It enhances existing relationships because it supports the free and truthful expression of feelings.

Turquoise

This gemstone helps to express thoughts clearly and truthfully in words. It is truly a communicator's stone.

When placed on the throat chakra, it is believed to help with the release from old and unnecessary vows that hold you back.

Aquamarine

This pale-blue to light green-blue stone connects one's consciousness with hidden emotions, allowing them to come into the open and be recognized and dealt with.

It helps to clear the mind and promotes honest communication.

It can also help speakers to overcome stage fright.

Angelite

Angelite brings compassion to the spoken word. It tempers truth with love and facilitates true connection between people, as well as between angels, guides, and people.

Azurite

This brilliant blue stone can be used for both the throat and the third eye chakras. It helps to resolve old and stagnant emotional issues, clearing their negative energy by allowing the words about them to be spoken.

Azurite was revered by several ancient civilizations.

It should be kept away from direct sunlight and out of heat; the mineral is soft and it loses its color in direct sun, while turning black when exposed to too much heat.

Blue Lace Agate

This stone emits a soft but powerful energy that is very effective to open and balance the throat chakra.

It can neutralize the effects of angry words and the hurt of feeling judged by others.

Blue lace agate enhances the courage to speak divine truths without hesitation.

Blue Kyanite

Blue kyanite can be used for any of the chakras, but its encouragement for self-expression makes it very suited to the throat chakra. It is a great aid in dealing with disagreements.

Kyanite doesn't need regular cleaning like other stones because it doesn't hold on to negativity.

Blue Apatite

Blue apatite is a deep blue stone that promotes open communication. It encourages speaking one's personal truth without negativity or anger.

The stone resonates with divine guidance and can stimulate intuition.

Sodalite

Sodalite emits a strong vibration that stimulates creativity, confidence, and the clear expression of thoughts.

It can also promote connections and friendships in business.

Aqua Aura Quartz

The flashing blue stone with rainbow luminescence contained deep within is a great aid to enhance communication and balance the throat chakra.

It will help you to recognize the right time to speak up for your truth and to verbalize your thoughts accurately.

Essential Oils and Herbs

Blackberry, elderberry, sage, lemongrass, laurel, eucalyptus, yarrow, blue chamomile, and frankincense will benefit the throat chakra.

Foods

The element of ether is light and insubstantial. The energies of the throat chakra are first on the road of formless existence. Color is more important than form and blue foods such as blueberries, blue grapes, and blackberries can be used.

Any fruits that grow on trees such as pears, apples, and plums are also beneficial to the throat chakra.

Soothing liquids such as raw honey and herbal teas will keep the throat chakra spinning efficiently.

In addition, Dr. Deepak Chopra's blog recommends taking one meal a day in silence and without any distractions such as reading or watching television, concentrating on chewing the food properly only (Easterly, 2020).

Affirmations

Here are a few suggestions for affirmations to get you started.

- I speak my truth freely and without fear.
- I embrace honesty to bring true freedom.
- I hold only myself accountable for expressing myself accurately.
- I allow others to speak their truth without interrupting them.
- My voice is powerful and clear.
- I speak and live with conviction and power.
- My words are always tempered by compassion.
- I trust other people.
- I am grounded and connected to my true self.
- I can easily contact my higher self for guidance.

A Guided Meditation

Use the following guided meditation to balance and heal your throat chakra and to live from its place of unconditional love.

Hold the gemstones or crystals for the throat chakra while you meditate, or arrange them around you. Build yourself a mandala by placing gemstones, herbs, and spices around or near you to enhance the effect of your meditation.

Record the script for this meditation on your cell phone to make meditating easy. Just remember to read slowly and give yourself enough time to move from step to step.

> *Find a comfortable position in a favorite chair, on a yoga mat, or a bed.*
> *Fold your hands loosely in your lap and keep your feet relaxed on the floor if you are sitting.*
> *If you are lying down, keep your legs straight and don't cross your ankles. Keep your arms next to your body on the bed or fold your hands over your midsection.*
> *Place a pillow under your knees if you need it for comfort.*
> *Close your eyes and visualize a tiny, spinning blue dot at the base of your throat. Feel it spinning in fresh air as you breathe in deeply and calmly.*
> *See the blue light expanding to your mouth and take another deep breath of its fresh air.*
> *See the blue glow growing to surround your whole body in freshness. Bathe in the ease with which you can breathe. Feel light and free.*
> *Guide the fresh, free, blue light back into your throat and see it coat your mouth, teeth, tongue, and vocal cords.*
> *Breathe in lightness...and exhale all heaviness.*
> *Savor the light and fresh feeling for as long as you like.*
> *[Pause]*
> *When you feel ready, stir your arms and legs and slowly become aware of the sounds of the outside world again.*

Open your eyes.

Music

Music specifically composed for balancing the throat chakra can be accessed freely at several places online. These include:

- https://www.youtube.com/watch?v=q5DUmjZDdQQ
- https://www.youtube.com/watch?v=lTHhkTQXw8I

Music in the key of D works for the throat chakra. Songs include "Another One Bites the Dust," by Queen, "God Rest Ye Merry, Gentlemen," by Mariah Carey, "That's All," by Genesis, "Feliz Navidad," by José Feliciano, "The Blue Danube Waltz," by Johann Strauss II, "Can't Help Falling in Love," by Elvis Presley, "Always on My Mind," by Willie Nelson, "Miss You Like Crazy," by Natalie Cole, "Time in a Bottle," by Jim Croce, and "You're in My Heart," by Rod Stewart.

Other Activities

As the throat chakra is about expressing your true self to others, a balancing activity would be something like starting a newsletter or a personal blog.

Any creative pastime such as drawing, painting, sculpting, doing pottery, or dancing also falls into this category.

Communicate your feelings in a letter or email to someone who's been on your mind a lot lately, or call them.

Get clear about your personal boundaries in relationships and speak out to establish them. Stand up for what is right and the things you believe in.

If you have an unresolved difference of opinion with anyone, talk to them and get the unpleasantness out of the air.

THE THIRD EYE CHAKRA—THE BRIDGE

The image for the third eye chakra.

SUMMARY

Sanskrit name: Ajna chakra
Color: Indigo blue

Seed mantra: Om

Location: Between the eyebrows

Element: Matter and energy

Gland: The pineal gland

Psychological function: Intelligence, intuition, insight, understanding, and self-knowledge.

THE SANSKRIT NAME

The Sanskrit word 'ajna' can be translated as 'perceiving' or "something beyond wisdom."

The Color

The midnight dark blue of this chakra is the color of thought and knowledge of the true self.

The Seed Mantra

The seed mantra for the third eye chakra is 'om.'

Location

It is located between the eyebrows, in the center of the forehead, as well as in the center of the skull.

Element

The third eye chakra is associated with the elements of energy and matter.

Gland

The third eye chakra relates to the pineal gland. This is a small, cone-shaped gland in the middle of the brain, close to the pituitary gland and the hypothalamus. The pineal gland regulates circadian rhythms through the production of melatonin.

Psychological function

A balanced third eye chakra gives an individual insight into the spiritual world and everything which is "beyond wisdom." It brings an assurance of the connection with the source of all things and dissolves all illusions of isolation.

UNDERSTANDING THE THIRD EYE CHAKRA

The third eye chakra is the door through which all the other chakras go to emerge into the spiritual realm. It lifts and clears all five the senses and transforms their energy into the higher vibrations of the Divine.

It brings clarity of thought and wisdom, as well the courage to express yourself freely.

A balanced and open third eye chakra brings supreme knowledge and understanding of the self, the world, and others. It creates harmony between body and mind and opens the way to fulfillment. Life's choices come easy because you are deeply connected to your inner voice. You know you can trust its guidance in all aspects.

THE SPIRITUAL LAW GOVERNING THE THIRD EYE CHAKRA

The spiritual law associated with the third eye chakra is the law of dharma. That refers to one's purpose in life.

It is about quieting the turmoil in the mind to hear the inner voice's counsel.

The Indian word 'dharma' includes several concepts, rather than just one thing, and there is no direct English translation for it. It refers to living according to one's unique and individual purpose in terms of divine law (Chopra, 2020a).

Every person has a unique gift to offer to the world. When you live true to the law of dharma, you seek until you find what your specific talents are and what your contribution to life should be.

It is about discovering your passions and the things that inspire you. When you work out how to use these things in the service of mankind, you can start living according to the law of dharma.

The utilization of your talents should be done with passion and joy. You must enter the natural, timeless flow of life where other people's opinions don't matter because you are in touch with divine guidance.

WHAT CAN BLOCK THE THIRD EYE CHAKRA?

Illness, emotional upsets, injuries to the head and face, and general disillusionment with life and relationships can all cause the third eye chakra to go out of balance or become completely blocked.

Exposure to heavy metals and fluoride, as well as a diet high in processed foods can also cause problems for this chakra.

SIGNS OF AN UNBALANCED THIRD EYE CHAKRA

The signs of a blocked third eye chakra include the following:

Physically

Headaches, blocked sinuses, blurred vision, aching eyes, hearing problems, insomnia, and even seizures can result when the third eye chakra is not open.

Psychologically

Confusion, uncertainty, a cynical outlook on life, an inability to access intuition, a sense of living without purpose, and pessimism are sure signs of a third eye chakra that is not functioning as it should.

RESTORING BALANCE AND HEALING THE THIRD EYE CHAKRA

Provided you have the intention and commitment to open and balance your chakra, there are several things you can do to help you achieve that.

Breathing Exercise

The technique known as kapalabhati pranayama, or skull-shining breath, is used to cleanse and open the third eye chakra. The Sanskrit word 'kapala' means skull, and 'bhati' means 'shining.'

Yogis believe a shining forehead is a sign of health. The shining head also symbolizes a clear and sharp intellect.

The technique works with a series of short, sharp inhalations.

Sit comfortably with your spine straight. Make sure your posture leaves room for free movement of your abdomen.

Unlike other breathing exercises that start on an inhalation, the exhalation is more important here. Exhale all your breath through your nose in one sharp, one-second burst. Keep your mouth closed.

Allow the automatic inhalation that follows and give yourself a second or two to rest before forcing the next exhalation out.

Repeat this cycle slowly until you get used to it. Then you can pick up the tempo by shortening the pauses between the ex and inhalations.

Aim to remove the pauses completely eventually, so you will inhale and exhale in rapid succession.

Become aware of a sensation of light in the area of the third eye, as well as a warm feeling throughout your body.

Continue the cycle for as long as you can—it is natural for your muscles to get tired in the beginning.

Release the exercise pattern with a long exhale. Inhale slowly and exhale again with a long sigh for a couple of times to normalize your breathing.

Aligning the sixth chakra with this technique will also benefit your crown chakra.

Nadi shodhana, or alternate nostril breathing, is another breathing pattern that can benefit the third eye chakra. See the chapter about the crown chakra for a full discussion of the technique.

Yoga

Practice these asanas, or poses, to help with balancing the third eye chakra:

Trataka/Candle Gazing

The third eye chakra is about perceiving the world in its totality, as well as its full and glorious truth.

The dancing flame of candle gazing sharpens your focus to go inward first, before gazing at the outer world with new perspectives.

- Sit in a comfortable position. It can be in a chair at a table or on your knees on a yoga mat.
- Place a lit candle in front of you at a distance from which you can look at the flame with an upright head and straight neck.
- Slightly unfocus your eyes and gaze intensely, without taking your eyes away at all, at the glow of the dancing flame until your eyes feel watery.
- Allow your eyelids to almost close.
- Pay attention to any feelings, visions, and flashes of insight that come to you while engaged in candle gazing.
- Finally, allow your eyes to close completely and focus on the after-image that remains—it could look like a little purple or red dot against your closed eyelids.
- Keep your candle gazing session up for two to three minutes.

Shirshasana/Headstand

The headstand is fully discussed in the chapter about the crown chakra. While it is an asana primarily aimed at the crown chakra, it also benefits the ajna chakra because the way toward the top of the head goes through the third eye.

The third eye benefits from the boosted blood circulation and renewed perspectives brought by regular headstands. The practice also relieves stress and enhances focus.

Remember to be very careful if you attempt this asana as a beginner. The safest way is to do it under the guidance of a yoga instructor. If you are on your own, do it near a wall for support.

Balasana/Child's Pose

The child's resting pose is an important stretch for several parts of the body. Moreover, it helps us to push pause in a hectic schedule and reflect on life for a few minutes. It allows you to reassess where you're at and decide on the way forward.

Use it when you feel a need to rest in body and/or mind.

If you have a knee injury, you should be careful when attempting this position. It should not hurt your knees.

- Start by kneeling on a yoga mat.
- Keep your hands flat on the mat before you.
- Spread your knees as wide as your mat, but keep your big toes touching and the tops of your feet flat on the mat.

- If keeping your feet flat hurts, you can curl your toes in instead.
- Your ankles should be relaxed; you can take some stress off them by placing a rolled towel under your shins.
- Bend forward far enough to rest your stomach between your thighs.
- Touch your forehead to the mat. If that is too uncomfortable for you, rest your head on two yoga blocks or a folded blanket.
- Be sure to find the 'reset' point that is located between your eyebrows and in the middle of your forehead. This point has to touch the mat or blocks for the vagus nerve to receive stimulation to provide a soothing "rest and digest" response.
- Relax your shoulders, neck, jaw, and face. Rather, support your neck with a blanket if you feel any pressure in the area.
- Hold your arms in a position that is comfortable for you. Listen to your body and do what it needs at the time. You can either stretch your arms and shoulders forward, palms down, or bring your arms to the back, next to your thighs, with your palms facing upward.
- Two other variations for arm positions are to stretch your arms forward with your palms facing upward to bring more release to your shoulders, or bend your elbows and rest your thumbs at the back of your neck.
- Keep the child's pose for as long as you need it.

Prasarita Padottanasana/Wide-legged Forward Fold

This is an inverted position that is somewhat more accessible to many people who cannot perform headstands.

If you have a back injury, it will be better to support your head on blocks or other props and not attempt to do the full bend.

- Stand on a yoga mat, facing the long edge.
- Move your feet apart as far as is comfortable for you. It can be any distance between three and four-and-a-half feet. Tall people should spread their legs a little wider than shorter folks.
- Keep your feet parallel to each other.
- Rest your hands on your hips.
- Press the outer edges of your feet and the balls of your big toes firmly down on the mat while lifting your inner arches.
- Draw your thigh muscles up firmly.
- Lift your chest on an inhalation so your front torso is slightly longer than the back, without bending backward.
- Exhale and bend your torso forward from the hips.
- Place your fingertips on the mat, in line with your shoulders, when your torso is parallel to the floor.
- Allow your back to be somewhat concave from your skull to your tailbone.
- Lift your head and move your gaze upward to the ceiling.
- Keep your pelvis as wide as possible.
- Take a few breaths while holding the position.
- The next step should only be attempted if you feel flexible

enough to bend further forward; do not stretch too much or injure yourself.
- On the next exhalation, walk your fingertips between your feet, bend your elbows, and lower your palms to the mat.
- That will put your head and torso into a full forward fold.
- If you can, bend low enough to allow the crown of your head to rest on the mat too.
- Yogis with advanced flexibility can also lower their forearms to rest on the mat.
- Stay in the pose for 30 seconds to one minute before rolling your body gently out of the position and back into an upright stance.

Mahasir Mudra/Mudra of the Great Head

This mudra is used to balance the energies of the mind and body. It counters the effects of stress and directs excess energy away from the head, toward the body.

- Curl your ring finger into your palm, so that the tip of your ring finger touches the crease at the base of your thumb.
- Touch the tips of your thumbs, index, and middle fingers together.
- Extend your pinkies.
- An optional step is to touch your right hand to the space between your eyebrows, so that the tips of the first three fingers touch your forehead.

Gemstones and Crystals

Several stones and crystals resonate with the third eye chakra.

Azurite

See the discussion about azurite in the chapter about the throat chakra.

Blue Aventurine

This is an excellent stone to clear stagnant negative energy and open the way for truth to shine through.

It brings the courage to be true to yourself to grow spiritually.

Labradorite/Spectrolite

This mineral is known as the stone of magic because of its powerful ability to stimulate and open deep connections. It enhances inner reflection and opens the door to higher consciousness.

Lapis Lazuli

See the discussion about lapis lazuli in the chapter about the throat chakra.

Sodalite

See the discussion about sodalite in the chapter about the throat chakra.

Iolite

Iolite can bring balance between our male and female energies, so our minds are free to concentrate on communication with the divine energy. It is a doorway to higher consciousness and its energies align perfectly with the third eye and crown chakras.

Iolite is also known as cordierite.

Amethyst

See the discussion about amethyst in the chapter about the crown chakra.

Fluorite

Fluorite can be found in several different colors. Although the purple variety is very effective to stimulate the third eye chakra, blue fluorite can enhance communication with divine energy to bring about spiritual awakening, while green fluorite can give intuition a boost.

The mineral brings mental sharpness and expands the mind to understand different viewpoints.

Pietersite

Pietersite is part of the tiger's eye family that is believed to stimulate the pineal gland. That puts the logical mind on the backburner, allowing spiritual truths and higher consciousness to take over.

It acts as a unification point for the sacral and solar plexus chakras. That enhances intuition and helps you see ways in which to bring your intuition into practical results in your life.

Pietersite is associated with storms and is a good booster for creativity.

Tanzanite

The high and strong vibration of tanzanite breaks open intuitive wisdom and perspectives. It brings a deep insight into everything in the universe, guiding you on the journey to reach your soul's purpose.

It links the energies of the third eye, throat, and heart chakras to bring upliftment after emotional losses and a general zest for life in all its facets.

Phenacite/Phenakite

Although phenacite is colorless, it emits a high vibration that is intensely stimulating to the third eye chakra.

It builds connections with the other chakras, working toward spiritual enlightenment.

It opens the communication channels with angels, guides, and ascended masters, as well as brings the ability to access information in the Akashic records.

The higher your own vibrations on your spiritual journey, the better you will resonate with phenacite.

Dumortierite

This is a rare mineral that soothes negativity and discomfort. It promotes harmony, self-discipline, and courage.

Essential Oils and Herbs

Lemon, sandalwood, rosemary, frankincense, German chamomile, eyebright, juniper, mugwort, poppy, and cypress can be used to activate and balance the third eye chakra.

Foods

The color of the third eye chakra is purple, and beneficial purple foods include grapes, eggplant, onion, cabbage, kale, figs, and carrots.

Add some foods that boost serotonin, to aid and calm an overworked mind, such as cocoa, eggs, tofu, and cheese.

Affirmations

Here are a few suggestions for affirmations to get you started.

- I trust my inner wisdom.
- I trust and follow my intuition.
- I am a divine light.
- I clearly receive guidance from the universe.
- I passionately seek the higher truth in all things.
- I recognize the divine being in other people.
- I function from unconditional and infinite love.
- Every situation is an opportunity for growth.
- I trust that everything is unfolding for my highest good.
- It comes naturally to me to see the bigger picture in all situations.

A Guided Meditation

Use the following guided meditation to balance and heal your third eye chakra and to live from its place of unconditional love.

Hold the third eye chakra gemstones or crystals while you meditate, or arrange them around you. Build yourself a mandala by placing gemstones, herbs, and spices around or near you to enhance the effect of your meditation.

Record the script for this meditation on your cell phone to make meditating easy. Just remember to read slowly and give yourself enough time to move from step to step.

> *Find a comfortable position in a favorite chair, on a yoga mat, or a bed.*
> *Fold your hands loosely in your lap and keep your feet relaxed on the floor if you are sitting.*
> *If you are lying down, keep your legs straight and don't cross your ankles. Keep your arms next to your body on the bed or fold your hands over your midsection.*
> *Place a pillow under your knees if you need it for comfort.*
> *Close your eyes and quiet your mind while visualizing a deeply soothing indigo light starting in the middle of your forehead.*
> *See the indigo light growing to fill your whole head.*
> *Watch the indigo glow folding around your whole body and be aware of a vast stillness that has entered your being...so peaceful...so soothing...so fulfilled.*

Feel all confusion and frustration flow out of your body to be replaced by the fulfilling, soothing indigo glow.
Become aware of being light as a feather...everything is effortless.
Breathe in peace...and exhale all confusion.
Savor the peace for as long as you like.
[Pause]
When you feel ready, stir your arms and legs and slowly become aware of the sounds of the outside world again.
Open your eyes.

Music

Music specifically composed for balancing the third eye chakra can be accessed freely at several places online. These include:

- https://www.youtube.com/watch?v=_T2WeP4uet4
- https://www.youtube.com/watch?v=dAAmGPvtqQE

Other pieces of music in the key of A can be used to open and balance the third eye chakra, such as "Buffalo Soldier," by Bob Marley, "Mrs. Robinson," by Simon and Garfunkel, "Hold the Line," by Toto, "Sweet Emotion," by Aerosmith, "Radar Love," by Golden Earring, "Maybe Baby," by Buddy Holly, "Tears in Heaven," by Eric Clapton, "Pié Jesu," by André Rieu, "Gloria," by Laura Branigan, and "So Long, Marianne," by Leonard Cohen.

Other Activities

Spend short but regular times in the sun to activate the chakras's element of light. When sunlight is in short supply, bask your third eye chakra in the inner light of meditation.

Start trusting your intuition. See if you can follow your gut instincts for one whole day. Listen to the needs of your body.

Expand your mental horizons by enrolling for a class in something that interests you, or learn a new language. Read up on different cultures and try to understand their way of life.

Keep a dream journal next to your bed and try to remember your dreams in the morning. Meditate on their meaning and listen to your inner voice.

8

THE CROWN CHAKRA—THE INFINITE

The image for the crown chakra.

SUMMARY

Sanskrit name: Sahasrara or brahamarandra chakra
Color: Violet/white

Seed mantra: Aum

Location: The top of the head

Element: Pure, divine consciousness

Gland: Pituitary and hypothalamus

Psychological function: Spirituality, enlightenment, dynamic thought, and energy

THE SANSKRIT NAME

The word sahasrara means 'infinite' or 'thousand.' It is associated with a lotus flower that has a thousand petals of different colors arranged in layers, signifying the diverseness of pure consciousness.

The lotus flower is a symbol of beauty growing from muddy, unlikely origins and despite unfavorable conditions.

The Color

Violet and white are seen as spiritual, royal colors. White is also associated with an open and active crown chakra.

Violet contains all the other colors in it and acts as a balance of all the chakras. It enables you to look beyond material values and a physical existence.

The Seed Mantra

The seed mantra for the crown chakra, 'aum,' is the primordial sound at the moment of creation.

Location

It is located above the top of the head, outside the body. It can be described as a meeting point between the body and the universe, where the body finds a bridge to the soul.

Element

The crown chakra is associated with the element of formless and pure consciousness that transcends the ego.

Gland

The pituitary gland and hypothalamus work together to regulate the endocrine system of the body. The endocrine system is a network of glands that regulate essential functions such as metabolism and body temperature.

Psychological Function

The effects of a balanced crown chakra are apparent in the individual's calm and compassionate behavior. There is no boredom, nameless melancholy, or disillusionment anymore. In their place, only peace, gratitude, and acceptance of our true selves remain.

UNDERSTANDING THE CROWN CHAKRA

When the crown chakra is open and energy can flow freely, we feel connected to the divine Source. We find flow and ease. We think of life in more positive terms and reject anything that creates stress.

THE SPIRITUAL LAW GOVERNING THE CROWN CHAKRA

The law of Pure Potentiality is the spiritual law that controls the seventh chakra.

This law goes into action as a result of a process that starts at the root chakra and develops with every chakra after that.

We receive our grounding and nourishment from the earth in the root chakra, get creative with the sacral chakra, form pure intentions and empower them in the solar plexus chakra, give and receive unconditional love from the heart chakra, express ourselves truthfully and with compassion from the throat chakra, and get back in touch with our inner, higher nature in the third eye chakra.

That journey culminates in our awareness of our infinite real nature, from the crown chakra. Then we remember again that everything is possible—there is pure potential all around us.

WHAT CAN BLOCK THE CROWN CHAKRA?

The biggest hurdle that can stand in the way of a balanced and fully functional crown chakra is an unwavering attachment to material objects and pursuits. The realm of the crown chakra is spiritual and mental, not physical and material.

SIGNS OF AN UNBALANCED CROWN CHAKRA

The signs of a blocked crown chakra include the following:

Physically

Poor coordination, excessive tiredness, chronic exhaustion, regular headaches, and neurological problems can be signs of an unbalanced crown chakra.

Psychologically

Depression, addictive behaviors, confusion, apathy, overwhelm, feeling unmotivated and directionless, difficulty to see another person's perspective, lack of empathy, and feelings of loneliness and isolation can be present.

RESTORING BALANCE AND HEALING THE CROWN CHAKRA

Meditation is your primary resource to balance and heal your crown chakra. It is also important to remember that the other six chakras have to be in balance too for the crown to function as it should.

Wear Purple

Surrounding and immersing yourself and your world in purple is a great way to start balancing this chakra. Wear the color when you can and add purple to your decor.

Journal

As with many of the other chakras, keeping a regular journal will help you find perspective on your life. Make it a habit to write down several things you are grateful for every day.

That will enhance your connection to the Creator, as well as your sense of security and feeling of being protected. You will appreciate life and the gifts from the universe more and develop respect for nature.

Volunteer

Getting out of your comfort zone to do volunteer work will lift you from the material world into the spiritual sphere. It will open your mind to the needs of others so you can see where you fit in.

That, in turn, will help you accept that you are deserving of happiness and good things too.

Breathing Exercise

Nadi shodhana, or alternate nostril breathing, is a simple technique that helps the mind to focus on the breath to open the crown chakra. Alternating the nostrils connects the two halves of the brain, bringing balance.

Place your thumb against your left nostril and breathe in through your right nostril. Now place the last two fingers of the same hand against your right nostril and breathe out through your left nostril.

Breathe in again through your left nostril before closing it with your thumb and breathing out through your right nostril.

Keep doing this for at least 10 repetitions, making sure you breathe in from the same nostril where you breathed out the last time.

Yoga

Practice these asanas, or poses, to help with balancing the crown chakra:

Shirshasana/Headstand

This yoga pose is often called the king of poses because it is done by balancing on the top of the head.

It is an advanced pose that should not be undertaken by anyone not ready for it or without supervision, preferably from a yoga instructor. It is safer to do the pose near a wall for support.

When done successfully, it improves the flow of oxygen-rich blood to the brain and speeds up blood circulation throughout the body.

- Sit on your knees with your thighs resting on your calves and your hands resting on your knees.
- Interlock your fingers and bend forward so that your forearms and the sides of your hands rest on the floor. There should be a triangle formation between your head and your arms and hands.
- Position the crown of your head against your interlocking fingers.

- Make sure your head is balanced firmly against your fingers and comfortable.
- Lift your knees and hips from the floor and straighten your legs.
- Slowly walk your feet closer to your body.
- Bend your knees and keep your heels close to your hips.
- Slowly straighten your hips.
- Straighten your knees and calves until your whole body is in a vertical position. Keep your feet relaxed. If you are a beginner with this pose, lift your legs one by one.
- Maintain the position for as long as you are comfortable. In the beginning, it need not be longer than a few seconds.
- Reverse the process to end the pose.
- Rest for a few minutes in the child's pose to recover your balance.

Sasangasana/Rabbit Pose

Rabbit pose is an excellent position to alleviate tension in the neck, shoulders, and back. It also increases blood flow to the nervous system that will support the thyroid and the whole endocrine system.

- Sit on your knees on the floor or a yoga mat, with your hips resting on your heels.
- Exhale and grab hold of your heels with your hands, palms facing outward. That means your thumbs will be facing toward the floor and your other fingers will be on the inside.
- Engaging your core muscles, round your back and put the

top of your head on the floor. That means your forehead will touch your knees and your crown will be on the floor.
- Lift your hips and move forward in a rolling motion until your elbows are locked in a straight line.
- Breathe deeply and enjoy the feeling of openness.
- Stay in the position for at least five breaths before coming up slowly, chin and head last.

Savasana/Corpse Pose

See the discussion of the corpse pose in the chapter on the root chakra.

Vrikshasana/Tree Pose

See the discussion of the tree pose in the chapter on the root chakra.

Ardha Padmasana/Half Lotus Pose

The half lotus pose is easier than full lotus because one foot remains on the ground. Some people will never be able to achieve full lotus without discomfort, and half lotus is a perfect substitute.

It helps the body and mind grow quiet enough to meditate and fully relax.

You can assume this position to chant the seed mantra of the crown chakra, 'aum.'

- Sit on the floor or yoga mat with your legs crossed.

- Lift your left foot out from under you and place it on top of your right thigh.
- Place your hands on your knees.
- Enjoy the stillness for as long as you like.

Sahasrara Mudra/Mudra of A Thousand Petals

Holding this mudra above your head will open the gateway for your crown chakra to function as it should.

- Hold your hands next to each other in front of you.
- Touch the tips of your thumbs and index fingers together to form a triangle.
- Turn your hands so that the other fingers point upward, keeping them straight.
- Raise the mudra above your head. Reach as high as is comfortable for you, but try for six to seven inches.
- Hold the position for between one and five minutes.

Gemstones and Crystals

Stones and crystals that resonate with the crown chakra are:

Amethyst

With its beautiful deep purple color, amethyst is one of the most spiritual stones in existence. It vibrates at a high frequency and acts as a bridge between the third eye chakra and the crown chakra. That opens the way for energy to flow freely to all the other chakras as well.

It can help to calm the mind and encourage reflection, focus, and intuition.

Selenite

This white stone is also sometimes referred to as "the doorway of the angels."

It helps to restore calm and reverse a depressed mood. Selenite encourages peace and brings feelings of security and lightness.

Sugilite

If you feel your circumstances are hopeless, blocking you from reaching enlightenment and understanding, use sugilite to restore your connection to Source energy.

That will make it possible for you to discern the lessons to be learned from your experiences, despite negative emotions.

Sugilite aligns all the chakras so you can put the lessons into practical applications for your life, too. Your self-belief and intuition will receive a boost, and you will grow in spiritual knowledge.

Lilac Spirit Quartz

Lilac quartz is a cluster crystal and it radiates energy in all directions. It is useful in group settings, such as family gatherings, to protect against negative energy.

The crystal boosts awareness of spiritual truths and enhances inner awareness.

Apophyllite

This stone is used as a link between the physical and spiritual worlds. It opens the heart and mind to light and love, and enhances spiritual development.

It can bring you closer to your spirit and animal guides.

The boosted intuition and wisdom acquired through the use of apophyllite break open truths about yourself and your spiritual journey that will be hard to ignore.

Charoite

Charoite aligns the crown with the heart chakra, promoting unconditional love and fulfilling your true and full potential.

It is a high energy stone that boosts mindfulness of the present moment and its gifts, even if they're disguised as challenges.

The stone also enhances focus and concentration.

Howlite

Howlite helps to cleanse the aura and calms the mind. It supports the release of emotional tension, anger, and mind chatter due to overwork.

In doing so, howlite is a great help in repairing disruptive sleep patterns. Adequate restful sleep is essential for a healthy and balanced crown chakra.

Tiffany Stone

This exquisite purple and white gem is made up of, among other minerals, bertrandite, traces of beryllium, clear quartz, and purple fluorite. It is also known as opal fluorite, purple passion, or ice cream stone.

It enables the connection between the third eye and crown chakras, opening the way for the free flow of spiritual guidance. It helps to clear the mind and release negative thoughts so that personal growth can continue.

White Calcite

White calcite also helps to clear the aura and assists in self-growth. It boosts motivation and renews hope, banishing stagnant energy from the auric field.

It is a stone that teaches forgiveness and paves the way for new beginnings.

Serpentine

Serpentine stimulates the crown chakra to boost confidence in one's own path rather than trying to conform to others' expectations.

It lays a foundation for deep meditation and introspection, leading to personal spiritual growth.

Lepidolite

The vibrations of this purple stone, often with white mica inclusions, are thought to increase the occurrence of synchronicities, or positive coincidences.

When lepidolite is used to activate the crown chakra, more white is desirable. A more solid purple stone is better as an aid to deep relaxation and meditation.

Scolecite

This stone is also classified as highly vibrational, able to assist with deep meditation and the cultivation of inner peace. It can open the communication channels with the universe and source energy.

Lapis Lazuli

See the discussion in the chapter about the throat chakra.

White Agate

This stone is associated with balance and the release of anger, frustration, and negativity. It balances the male and female sides of the personality.

It stimulates the crown chakra and attracts spirit helpers and guides.

Essential Oils and Herbs

The oils of lavender, rose, vetiver, spikenard, sandalwood, cedarwood, lemon, sage, juniper, and frankincense, palo santo, frangipani,

Chinese rice flower, and white lotus flower all have powerful effects on the crown chakra.

Foods

The focus of the crown chakra is more spiritual than physical. Fasting, rather than food, is therefore better to open and balance the crown chakra. Detoxing, regular meditation, and calming yoga will be very beneficial.

Affirmations

Here are a few suggestions for affirmations to get you started.

- I am one with the universe.
- All the levels of my being are integrated.
- I am deeply at peace.
- I remove all limiting beliefs and blocks.
- Infinite possibilities beckon me.
- I easily tap into my inner wisdom.
- I accept and receive gratefully the energy flowing through my chakras.
- I understand my life's purpose.
- I love and accept myself fully.
- I am a divine being.

A Guided Meditation

Use the following guided meditation to balance and heal your crown chakra and to live from its place of unconditional love.

Hold the crown chakra gemstones or crystals while you meditate, or arrange them around you. Build yourself a mandala by placing gemstones, herbs, and spices around or near you to enhance the effect of your meditation.

Record the script for this meditation on your cell phone to make meditating easy. Just remember to read slowly and give yourself enough time to move from step to step.

> *Find a comfortable position in a favorite chair, on a yoga mat, or a bed.*
> *Fold your hands loosely in your lap and keep your feet relaxed on the floor if you are sitting.*
> *If you are lying down, keep your legs straight and don't cross your ankles. Keep your arms next to your body on the bed or fold your hands over your midsection.*
> *Place a pillow under your knees if you need it for comfort.*
> *Close your eyes and imagine a calm purple glow surrounding your head.*
> *See the glow sprouting upward in a stalk.*
> *See the stalk forming a bud…and see the bud transforming into a brilliant purple lotus with a thousand perfectly formed petals, opening them up to send out a heavenly fragrance.*
> *See a shaft of white light coming down toward the lotus and entering it, filling your head and your body with light, peace, love, and understanding.*
> *See the white light moving through your body, swirling around every chakra and spinning it joyfully and with love.*

Know you are one with the divine.
Breathe in unity...and exhale isolation.
Savor the feeling for as long as you like.
[Pause]
When you feel ready, stir your arms and legs and slowly become aware of the sounds of the outside world again.
Open your eyes.

Music

Music specifically composed for balancing the crown chakra can be accessed freely at several places online. These include:

- https://www.youtube.com/watch?v=HojZD4IpRR0
- https://www.youtube.com/watch?v=5xGlzxU8rew

Besides the balancing melodies available for listen and download online, any songs in the musical key of B resonate well with the crown chakra.

Examples of songs include "Sweet Caroline," by Neil Diamond, "The Boxer," by Simon and Garfunkel, "Revolution," by The Beatles, "Brothers in Arms," by Dire Straits, "Born in the USA," by Bruce Springsteen, "What's Love Got to Do With It," by Tina Turner, "Someday Never Comes," by Creedence Clearwater Revival, "Angel," by Rod Stewart, "Rainy Day People," by Gordon Lightfoot, and "O Holy Night," by Adolphe Adam.

Other Activities

The best thing you can do for the health of your crown chakra is to meditate. It does not have to be long sessions—five or ten minutes to start with will be enough. Just get into the habit of regular meditation.

Make time for activities that relax you and bring you in contact with that "quiet voice within." Schedule a regular massage or book an acupuncture or aromatherapy treatment.

CONCLUSION

We have come to the end of an exciting journey through the world of chakras. You are now equipped with all the knowledge you need to keep yours fully open and balanced.

When life happens and any chakra goes out of balance, you will also be able to recognize the problem and know which steps to take to rectify the situation.

May you experience a life lived to the fullest potential through the application of the techniques presented in this book.

REVIEW

Did you enjoy the book? Did the information enhance your life quality and aid you on your personal spiritual journey?

If so, please leave a positive review on Amazon, so others can find the book too and experience its benefits.

REFERENCES

Alcantara, M. (2017). Chakra healing : A beginner's guide to self-healing techniques that balance the chakras. Althea Press.

Ancillette, M. (n.d.-a). 9 sacral chakra crystals and stones for healing the 2nd chakra. Angel Grotto. https://angelgrotto.com/crystals-stones/sacral-chakra/

Ancillette, M. (n.d.-b). Crown chakra stones: 10 of the best crystals for the sahasrara. Angel Grotto. https://angelgrotto.com/crystals-stones/crown-chakra/

Ancillette, M. (2020). 9 best healing stones & crystals for the root chakra. Angel Grotto. https://angelgrotto.com/crystals-stones/root-chakra/

Aragon, D. L. (2011, September 2). Chakras of the American Indians. Www.edgarcayce.org. https://www.edgarcayce.org/about-us/blog/blog-posts/chakras-of-the-american-indians/

Art of Living. (n.d.). Triangle pose-how to do trikonasana. Art of Living (Global). https://www.artofliving.org/yoga/yoga-poses/triangle-pose-trikonasana

Bartz, J. (2016, August 16). 6 yoga poses to give you more energy & ignite your creativity. Mindbodygreen. https://www.mindbodygreen.com/0-26221/6-yoga-poses-to-give-you-more-energy-ignite-your-creativity.html

Besser, B. (2007). Synopsis of the historical development of Schumann resonances. Radio Science, 42(2), n/a. https://doi.org/10.1029/2006rs003495

Boyd, L. (2020, August 6). Five asanas to stimulate the heart chakra. Balance.media. https://balance.media/heart-chakra-asanas/

Cape Cod Crystals. (2021). Stones for the root chakra. Cape Cod Crystals. https://capecodcrystals.com/pages/root-chakra-stones-healing-crystals-for-the-root-chakra

Caron, M. (2018, November 5). Healing the root chakra with food. Sivana East. https://blog.sivanaspirit.com/hl-sp-root-chakra-food/

Cavill, A. (2019, August 27). Best yoga poses to open your crown chakra sahasrara. Www.yogadownload.com. https://www.yogadownload.com/best-yoga-poses-to-open-your-crown-chakra-sahasrara

Chopra, D. (2013, December 11). What everyone needs to know about their chakras. Mindbodygreen. https://www.mindbodygreen.com/0-11943/what-everyone-needs-to-know-about-their-chakras.html

Chopra, D. (2020a, January 29). Deepak Chopra explains the law of dharma and purpose in life. The Joy Within. https://thejoywithin.org/authors/deepak-chopra/the-law-of-dharma-and-purpose-in-life

Chopra, D. (2020b, October 27). The law of least effort is the 4th spiritual law of success. InnerSelf. https://innerself.com/personal/happiness-and-self-help/performance/3968-law-of-least-effort-by-deepak-chopra.html

Crystal Herbs. (n.d.). A guide to the subtle energy bodies & points. Www.crystalherbs.com. https://www.crystalherbs.com/aura-subtle-bodies.asp

Duggal, N. (2018, August 23). Pineal gland function: What you should know. Healthline. https://www.healthline.com/health/pineal-gland-function#:~:text=The%20pineal%20gland%20is%20a

Easterly, E. (2020, June 16). Eating to balance your chakras. Chopra. https://www.chopra.com/articles/eating-to-balance-your-chakras

Fellows, E. (n.d.). Traveling the energetic highway: What are meridians? Www.centerpointhealing.com. https://www.centerpointhealing.com/hyattsville/traveling-the-energetic-highway-what-are-meridians/#:~:text=The%20simplest%20definition%20is%20that

Feuerstein, G. (2003). The deeper dimension of yoga: Theory and practice. Shambhala.

Frawley, D. (n.d.). Opening the chakras: New myths & old truths. Yogainternational.com. https://yogainternational.com/article/view/opening-the-chakras-new-myths-old-truths

Gibson, L. (2020, January 5). Yoga's energy centers: What science says about the chakras. Yogauonline.com. https://yogauonline.com/yoga-research/yogas-energy-centers-what-science-says-about-chakras

Jain, R. (n.d.-a). Half bridge pose–ardha setubandhasana. Arhanta Yoga Ashram. https://www.arhantayoga.org/half-bridge-pose-ardha-setubandhasana/

Jain, R. (n.d.-b). Plough pose - Halasana. Arhanta Yoga Ashram. https://www.arhantayoga.org/plough-pose-halasana/

Jain, R. (n.d.-c). Shoulderstand – Sarvangasana. Arhanta Yoga Ashram. https://www.arhantayoga.org/shoulderstand-sarvangasana/

Jain, R. (2020a, August 24). Muladhara chakra, root chakra - Complete guide. Arhanta Yoga Ashram. https://www.arhantayoga.org/blog/all-you-need-to-know-about-muladhara-chakra-root-chakra/

Jain, R. (2020b, August 26). Svadhishthana-Sacral chakra: All you need to know. Arhanta Yoga Ashram. https://www.arhantayoga.org/blog/svadhishthana-chakra-all-you-need-to-know-about-the-sacral-chakra/

Jain, R. (2020c, October 7). Ajna chakra your third-eye chakra awakening. Arhanta Yoga Ashram. https://www.arhantayoga.org/blog/ajna-chakra-your-third-eye-chakra-awakening/

Jain, R. (2020d, October 8). Crown chakra: The divine energy of sahasrara chakra. Arhanta Yoga Ashram. https://www.arhantayoga.org/blog/crown-chakra-divine-energy-of-sahasrara-chakra/

Jodie. (2021, January 3). Reiki — universal life energy. Medium. https://medium.com/beingwell/reiki-universal-life-energy-4fb143b279a

Kazanis, Dr. D. (1995). The physical basis of subtle bodies and near-death experiences. Journal of Near-Death Studies, 14(2). https://doi.org/10.17514/jnds-1995-14-2-p101-116.

Kerkar, P. (2017, August 30). 10 myths about chakras healing. EPainAssist. https://www.epainassist.com/chakra/10-myths-about-chakras-healing

La Forge, T. (2016, June 17). Food and chakra pairing: Balancing and healing our energy centers through food. Parsnips and Pastries. https://www.parsnipsandpastries.com/chakra-food-pairing-balancing-healing-energy-centers-food/

Leatherbury, H. (2018, November 24). 5 yoga practices to balance the third eye chakra. YogiApprovedTM. https://www.yogiapproved.com/yoga/third-eye-chakra-yoga-practices/

Lee, C. (2010, December 8). Learn How to Come Into Uttanasana (Standing Forward Bend) Safely. Yoga Journal. https://www.yogajournal.com/practice/beginners/standing-forward-bend/

Leigh, J. (2019). Etheric body. Energy Healing Institute. https://energyhealinginstitute.org/etheric-body/

Liforme. (n.d.). 4 yoga poses to clear the vishuddha (throat) chakra. Liforme. https://liforme.com/blogs/blog/yoga-poses-clear-vishuddha-throat-chakra

Magdalena, A. (2020, May 16). Best 9 crystals for the heart chakra. Gemstagram. https://gemstagram.com/crystals-for-heart-chakra/

Mansy, J. (2016, October 5). Spirituality, Sufism & Starbucks: Islam's chakra system. MissMuslim. https://missmuslim.nyc/spirituality-sufism-and-starbucks-islams-chakra-system/

Martinez, D. (2007, August 28). Half Lord of the Fishes pose (Ardha Matsyendrasana). Yoga Journal. https://www.yogajournal.com/poses/types/twists/half-lord-of-the-fishes-pose/

Maxwell, R. W. (2009). The physiological foundation of yoga chakra expression. Zygon(R), 44(4), 807–824. https://doi.org/10.1111/j.1467-9744.2009.01035.x

Neuenfeldt, K. (1998). The quest for a "magical island": The convergence of the didjeridu, aboriginal culture, healing and cultural politics in new age discourse. Social Analysis: The International Journal of Anthropology, 42(2), 73–102.

New World Encyclopedia. (2021, April 28). Chakra. Www.newworldencyclopedia.org. https://www.newworldencyclopedia.org/entry/Chakra

Nguyen, J. (2014, February 19). How to do rabbit pose. DoYou. https://www.doyou.com/how-to-do-rabbit-pose/

Norris, R. (2020, April 1). 8 stretches to help open up your heart chakra during stressful times. Well+Good. https://www.wellandgood.com/heart-chakra-open/

Oakes, L. (n.d.). A to Z of crystals, minerals, and stones. HealingCrystalsForYou.com. https://www.healing-crystals-for-you.com/a-to-z-of-crystals-minerals-and-stones.html

Perrakis, A. (2018). The ultimate guide to chakras : The beginner's guide to balancing, healing, and unblocking your chakras for health and positive energy. Fair Winds Press, An Imprint Of The Quarto Group.

Pizer, A. (2020a, July 5). Tackle your first yoga balance safely with tree pose. Verywell Fit. https://www.verywellfit.com/tree-pose-vrksasana-3567128

Pizer, A. (2020b, July 5). The importance of savasana: Learning how to rest your mind. Verywell Fit. https://www.verywellfit.com/corpse-pose-savasana-3567112

Pizer, A. (2020c, July 28). How do you do tadasana, yoga's mountain pose? Verywell Fit. https://www.verywellfit.com/mountain-pose-tadasana-3567127

Prana Yoga. (2014, June 3). Shashankasana–hare posture & balasana–child's posture. Pranayoga.co.in. https://pranayoga.co.in/asana/shashankasana-hare-posure-balasana-childs-posture/

Regan, S. (2020, July 16). 6 ways to balance your sacral chakra. Mindbodygreen. https://www.mindbodygreen.com/0-5332/6-Ways-to-Balance-Your-Sacral-Chakra.html

Rice, A. (2020, January 3). 7 mudras to unlock your 7 chakras. Mindbodygreen. https://www.mindbodygreen.com/0-20543/7-mudras-to-unlock-your-7-chakras.html

Riess, A. (2019). Dark matter. In Encyclopædia Britannica. https://www.britannica.com/science/dark-matter

Sadhguru. (2018, August 4). Muladhara chakra: Stabilizing the foundation. Isha Sadhguru. https://isha.sadhguru.org/in/en/wisdom/article/muladhara-chakra

Sadhguru. (2021, January 8). 7 chakras: Mystical dimensions of the body's seven chakras. Isha Sadhguru. https://isha.sadhguru.org/in/en/wisdom/article/7-chakras-mystical-dimensions-body-seven-chakras

Singh, J. (n.d.). Why do the chakras get blocked? (Symptoms of blocked chakras). Mindfulness Quest. https://mindfulnessquest.com/why-do-the-chakras-get-blocked/

Southgate, N. (n.d.). Chakradance chakra healing and balancing practice. Www.chakradance.com. https://www.chakradance.com/the-chakradance-practice

Steffgen, K. A. (2013, October 9). Boost your energy and fire up your passion with sacral chakra. Change Your Energy. https://www.changeyourenergy.com/blog/686/20131009-boost-your-energy-and-fire-up-your-passion-with-sacral-chakra

Stelter, G. (2016, October 4). A beginner's guide to the 7 chakras and their meanings. Healthline; Healthline Media. https://www.healthline.com/health/fitness-exercise/7-chakras

Stokes, V. (2021, February 17). Essential oils for chakras: Balance and heal with scents. Healthline. https://www.healthline.com/health/essential-oils-for-chakras#oils-and-chakras

Swami Nishchalananda. (2020, June 1). The chakras in traditions worldwide – a synopsis. Swami Nishchalananda. https://swami-nishchalananda.com/2020/06/01/the-chakras-in-traditions-worldwide-a-synopsis/

Tamara. (2011, April 13). Chakras: Your body's energetic system. Www.allyuspa.com. https://www.allyuspa.com/2011/chakras-your-bodys-energetic-system/

The Art of Living. (n.d.). Sirsasana: The yogic headstand. Art of Living (India). https://www.artofliving.org/in-en/yoga/yoga-poses/head-stand-sirsasana

The Joy Within. (2019, February 20). How to do kapalabhati pranayama: Skull-shining breath. The Joy Within. https://thejoywithin.org/breath-exercises/how-to-do-kapalabhati-pranayama-skull-shining-breath

Thomason, K. (2017, September 14). These 3 moves will help you finally master crow pose. Women's Health. https://www.womenshealthmag.com/fitness/a19932355/how-to-do-crow-pose/

Through the Phases. (2019, November 22). 20 powerful root chakra affirmations to get grounded. Through the Phases. https://www.throughthephases.com/powerful-root-chakra-affirmations/

Through the Phases. (2020, May 1). 20 powerful solar plexus affirmations to develop your purpose. Through the Phases. https://www.throughthephases.com/solar-plexus-affirmations/

Van Laer, L., & Lloyd, R. (n.d.). Mayan yoga: Chakras and energy in ancient middle America. http://www.doremishock.com/manuscripts/Mayanyoga.pdf

Vibrant Yogini. (2018, May 13). The ultimate guide for opening the heart chakra. Vibrant Yogini. https://www.vibrantyogini.com/the-ultimate-guide-for-opening-heart-chakra/#Heart_Chakra_Meditation_Pranayama_(breathing_exercise)

Wang, M., & Pregadio, F. (2011). Foundations of internal alchemy: The taoist practice of neidan. Golden Elixir Press.

Wimmer, R. (2012, December 1). Consciousness: Ayurvedic Medicine, Chinese Medicine, and Mayan Perspectives. Www.acupuncturetoday.com. https://www.acupuncturetoday.com/mpacms/at/article.php?id=32672#:~:text=Chinese%20Medicine%20Perspective&text=Chakras%20are%20articulated%20within%20Chinese

Yoga Journal. (2007, August 28). Warrior II pose (Virabhadrasana II). Yoga Journal. https://www.yogajournal.com/poses/warrior-ii-pose/

Yogapedia. (n.d.). Yogapedia. Www.yogapedia.com. https://www.yogapedia.com

Yogateket. (2019, June 18). Pranayama for Root Chakra. Yogateket. https://yogateket.com/blog/pranayama-for-root-chakra

Images

Altmann, G. (2016). Emotions are always reflected in our bodies. In Pixabay. https://pixabay.com/illustrations/woman-silhouette-meditation-clouds-1927662/

Hassan, M. (2020). The locations of all the chakras. In Pixabay. https://pixabay.com/vectors/chakra-meditation-aura-energy-5628622/

Johnson, G. (2017). Some people use yoga as an attempt to find a physical relationship between our bodies and chakras. In Pixabay. https://pixabay.com/vectors/yoga-typography-type-text-words-2099080/

Lomas, P. (2017a). The image for the crown chakra. In Pixabay. https://pixabay.com/illustrations/crown-chakra-energy-chi-spiritual-2533113/

Lomas, P. (2017b). The image for the heart chakra. In Pixabay. https://pixabay.com/illustrations/heart-chakra-energy-chi-spiritual-2533104/

Lomas, P. (2017c). The image for the root chakra. In Pixabay. https://pixabay.com/illustrations/root-chakra-energy-chi-spiritual-2533091/

Lomas, P. (2017d). The image for the sacral chakra. In Pixabay. https://pixabay.com/illustrations/sacral-chakra-energy-chi-spiritual-2533094/

Lomas, P. (2017e). The image for the solar plexus chakra. In Pixabay. https://pixabay.com/illustrations/solar-chakra-chi-energy-spiritual-2533097/

Lomas, P. (2017f). The image for the third eye chakra. In Pixabay. https://pixabay.com/illustrations/brow-chakra-energy-chi-spiritual-2533110/

Lomas, P. (2017g). The image for the throat chakra. In Pixabay. https://pixabay.com/illustrations/throat-chakra-chi-energy-spiritual-2533108/

Printed in Great Britain
by Amazon